JOYFUL LEARNING

SECOND EDITION

JOYFUL LEARNING

Active and Collaborative Strategies for Inclusive Classrooms

SECOND EDITION

Alice Udvari-Solner
Paula Kluth

CORWIN
A SAGE Publishing Company

CORWIN
A SAGE Publishing Company

FOR INFORMATION:

Corwin
A SAGE Company
2455 Teller Road
Thousand Oaks, California 91320
(800) 233-9936
www.corwin.com

SAGE Publications Ltd.
1 Oliver's Yard
55 City Road
London EC1Y 1SP
United Kingdom

SAGE Publications India Pvt. Ltd.
B 1/I 1 Mohan Cooperative Industrial Area
Mathura Road, New Delhi 110 044
India

SAGE Publications Asia-Pacific Pte. Ltd.
3 Church Street
#10-04 Samsung Hub
Singapore 049483

Program Director: Jessica Allan
Senior Associate Editor: Kimberly Greenberg
Senior Editorial Assistant: Katie Crilley
Production Editor: Veronica Stapleton Hooper
Copy Editor: Amy Hanquist Harris
Typesetter: Hurix Systems Pvt. Ltd.
Proofreader: Barbara Coster
Indexer: Molly Hall
Cover Designer: Anupama Krishnan
Marketing Manager: Charline Maher

Printed in the United States of America

Library of Congress Cataloging-in-Publication Data

Names: Udvari-Solner, Alice, author. | Kluth, Paula, author.

Title: Joyful learning : active and collaborative strategies for inclusive classrooms / Alice Udvari-Solner, Paula Kluth.

Description: Second edition. | Thousand Oaks : Corwin, [2017] | Includes bibliographical references and index.

Identifiers: LCCN 2017014861 | ISBN 9781506375663 (pbk. :acid-free paper)

Subjects: LCSH: Inclusive education—United States. | Activity programs in education—United States.

Classification: LCC LC1201 .U38 2017 | DDC 371.9/0460973—dc23 LC record available at https://lccn.loc.gov/2017014861

This book is printed on acid-free paper.

SFI® Certified Sourcing
www.sfiprogram.org
SFI-00453

17 18 19 20 21 10 9 8 7 6 5 4 3 2 1

Contents

Preface

In our work in inclusive schools, we often talk to teachers about a variety of ways they can develop curriculum and instruction to be more responsive to the diverse learners in their classrooms. For many reasons, one of the practices we feel is the most "tried and true" for achieving this goal is the use of active and collaborative learning.

One reason we promote this type of instruction is related to student response. We find that students (including those in our own university classrooms) react very positively to active and collaborative learning techniques and that this type of teaching lends itself well to universal lesson design, differentiation, and individualization of instruction. Furthermore, in our observation, students are more engaged and seemingly comprehend more when they have agency in the learning process.

We are also drawn to instruction that is interactive and multilevel because research indicates that all students, including those with disabilities, learn better when they are able to make meaning and demonstrate what they know in authentic ways. In fact, a multiyear study that Alice (the first author of this text) conducted about educators' responses to diverse learners indicated that when teachers created more responsive classrooms by changing lesson formats, teaching strategies, and instructional arrangements, the engagement, participation, and interactions of students with significant disabilities increased significantly (Udvari-Solner, 1995).

Research and related literature indicate that other populations such as students with identified gifts and talents, those from diverse cultural backgrounds, and learners at the college level also benefit from active and responsive classrooms, showing increased interest, retention of material, and levels of participation (Beichner, 2014; Bonwell & Eisen, 1991; Cole, 2001; Freeman et al., 2014; Harry & Klingner, 2005; Hohmann, Epstein, & Wiekart, 2008; Johnson, D. W., Johnson, & Smith, 1998; Marzano, 2003; Prince, 2004; Tomlinson, 2003).

We are also interested in this work because of the students sitting in classrooms today; we are now teaching the millennial and postmillennial generations (Wilson & Gerber, 2008). These students who have been born into the digital age of information, technology, and social networking pose new learning preferences and needs (Prensky, 2001). Notably, the teaching approaches that are preferred by and recommended for millennials are group oriented, highly active, variety-filled, and attend to the social aspects of learning—exactly the strategies we advocate in this book (Prensky, 2010; Roehl, Linga Reddy, & Shannon, 2013).

Finally, we feel that these strategies are helpful in supporting one more group: professionals. These structures make our work more interesting and more enjoyable. They inspire laughter. They make the classroom more fun. They help us meet the needs of a wider range of students. They also inspire us to team with our colleagues in a range of ways. When we use active and collaborative learning structures in elementary and secondary classrooms, it is easy to plan ways for related service providers (e.g., speech therapists, occupational therapists), fellow classroom teachers (e.g., English language [EL] professionals, general and special educators), and paraprofessionals to coteach and support all students. When students engage in a very busy and social structure such as *Dinner Party* (p. 80), for instance, we often ask speech therapists to work with small groups on pragmatics and vocabulary development. When we use text-based techniques such as *Say Something* (p. 122), we often collaborate with reading specialists, asking them to work with different groups of students throughout the lesson so that all learners can gain more powerful comprehension strategies.

For all of these reasons, we began collecting active and collaborative learning structures and working with practicing educators and preservice teachers to adapt these different structures to meet the needs of a wider variety of students. As we shared these techniques in our classes and inservice presentations, teachers and university students alike asked us where they could find more information on using the structures in their inclusive classes. For instance, they wanted to use *Dinner Party,* but they were curious about how to use it in a classroom where one or two students used augmentative communication systems. They were interested in *Say Something,* but were unsure how to use it with a student who was an emerging reader. These requests led us to develop this resource, which includes active learning techniques appropriate for use in K–12 classrooms and beyond. We explicitly designed structures that allow a wide range of students to participate, contribute, learn, collaborate with peers, and succeed.

Although some of the structures featured are not new in the sense that we created or named them (in fact, a number are purposely included because they are already popular with teachers and used widely in elementary and secondary classrooms), we feel this book is unique in that many texts related to active learning, differentiated instruction, or universal design do not include information or ideas appropriate for some inclusive classrooms; contain few examples related to learners with disabilities— especially those with significant disabilities; and lack specific suggestions for designing activities for the range of learners in a typical class. Alternatively, *Joyful Learning* focuses explicitly on inclusive classrooms; provides unique suggestions for meeting the needs of students with disabilities, including those with learning, intellectual, physical, and sensory differences; contains dozens of familiar and novel activities that all students can access; and illustrates ways all students can participate in them.

Using This Book

The activities in this book are clearly intended for or are at least well suited for use in classrooms in which students may have marked differences in ability, need, language, culture, or learning profile. We are hoping that by creating this resource, we are also promoting the idea that students with such differences can and should learn side by side.

How the Text Is Organized

The introduction to the book explores how inclusive schooling, differentiated instruction, and active learning are (or should be) linked and related. The five chapters that follow describe 60 structures that can be used with students in both elementary and secondary schools, and in a final note at the very end of the book, we reflect on the nature of joyful learning with recommendations for its cultivation in the classroom.

Please note that we have attempted to organize the structures into logical categories to help the reader locate techniques that match an instructional purpose. However, we don't believe the categories are mutually exclusive, and many structures can be employed for multiple instructional uses. Therefore, consider the chapter headings simply as a guide. The five chapters are as follows:

1. **"Building Teams and Classroom Communities."** This initial chapter includes techniques that help teachers build community and teaming. These structures promote relationship building, listening, sharing, and interdependence.

2. **"Teaching and Learning."** This chapter contains structures that help students of all ages learn standards-based content in meaningful, interesting, and compelling ways. This collection of ideas will help learners remember information, teach content to one another, and make discoveries about course content.

3. **"Studying and Reviewing."** The study and review structures give teachers ideas for supporting students as they work independently or with small groups to prepare for assessments or learn familiar content in a deeper way.

4. **"Creating Active Lectures."** Every teacher needs to engage in whole-class instruction and lecture-based instruction at some point during the school day. This instruction does not need to be formal and dry, however. By using the structures outlined in this chapter, teachers can involve their students in whole-class learning without losing those who need a more dynamic or personalized approach.

5. **"Assessing and Celebrating."** Structures offered in this chapter will give educators active-learning options for assessing student understanding, encouraging learners to teach and share, and celebrating growth.

Each one of these chapters features 12 activities. Each structure is outlined in detail with directions, reproducible handouts (when applicable), classroom-tested examples, and guidelines for maximizing the participation of students. Some structures also feature tips for implementation and ideas for extending or varying the structure. Each description is followed by space to record notes and ideas for using the structure in your classroom. We encourage you to log how you used the structure and then reflect on any of the following elements:

- Did the students learn what I had intended?

- Were the students able to carry out the structure, or are changes needed in the way I organized it or provided directions?

- Were all students engaged?

- What additional changes might be needed to maximize engagement and participation for particular students?

- If coteaching with another adult, how can we facilitate or guide our students more effectively as a team?

- Where else in my teaching can I use this strategy?

Using the Structures

This book is best used as a coplanning tool between general educators and specialists (e.g., special educators, EL educators, occupational therapists, speech therapists, physical therapists). We recommend that all team members who share responsibility for the same students become familiar with the structures and the associated procedures. In our research, we found that when members of educational teams used the same language and understood the same techniques, joint planning for differentiation was expedited (Udvari-Solner, 1996a). Effective supports for students with learning differences occur when instructional teams meet on a consistent basis (i.e., weekly or biweekly) and determine what is important for students to learn and how best to organize that learning. Familiarity with the structures in this book by all team members will provide an abundance of options for reaching those students who challenge us the most as educators.

If you don't currently have strong collaborative partnerships, using these structures can be an effective way to begin such a relationship. In our preservice courses, we often suggest that special educators or therapists seeking to coteach or to further develop their inclusive education model should offer to demonstrate active and collaborative structures as a way into the general education classroom. A general education classroom teacher who seems less than enthusiastic about making changes in curriculum or instruction can often be inspired to do so when alternatives to traditional teaching are not only suggested but also modeled. Such an offer illustrates that all adults in the building can and should teach and design instruction and that it is not just the job of the general educator to take on new roles.

Having shared how important it is for teaching teams to use these structures, we can now turn to another important group of instructors: students. We feel strongly that as educators we are modeling techniques that we want students to use and incorporate into their own instructional repertoire. There may be times when it is appropriate for a student or group of students to lead a class discussion or present reports or individual research. These techniques can be used to enliven this process and give students yet another arena for building skills and developing competencies.

Administrators are yet another audience for this material. If you are a principal, department chairperson, or even superintendent, consider using these structures in your meetings and staff development activities. Because teachers are learners too, you are likely to get a higher quality of participation in meetings when you are using techniques that will reach and interest larger numbers of "students." Further, there is no better way to emphasize a commitment to and enthusiasm for active and collaborative learning than to model it in your own work. For instance, a middle school principal had his staff try out the *Group Résumé* activity (p. 22) during a summer staff development institute. Teachers were mixed into groups with those from different grade levels and specialty areas and asked to construct the résumé on large pieces of chart paper. This activity gave the teachers the opportunity to learn about the skills and competencies of one another and, ultimately, helped them get and give support to one another on topics ranging from cooperative learning to flipping classrooms to conducting classroom meetings to developing a schoolwide service learning program. The résumés were then posted around the room and used as springboards for the next activity, which was to develop an action plan for learning from colleagues.

Finally, consider this book as a vehicle for professional development. As authors, we have been asked by innumerable school districts and organizations to work with specific teaching teams or entire buildings or districts to learn and integrate these strategies into daily practice. Teaching has been called one of the loneliest professions, and unfortunately—in some schools—trying something new in the classroom can feel risky. We believe there is strength in numbers and that being creative in the classroom should be supported and celebrated in the school community. In healthy organizations, new information and innovative practices are shared in collaborative ways. One way to facilitate this shift in school culture is to initiate professional development that focuses on the use of active and collaborative structures to differentiate instruction or inspire the universal design of lessons.

This type of staff development can be as simple as a book study group or as organized as a formal action research project. Some schools with which we have worked arranged for a group of interested faculty to meet weekly or biweekly to read and discuss the ideas in this book. In these groups, teachers select structures of interest and agree to implement one or two within the week. In each subsequent meeting, teachers share their successes and challenges. This informal arrangement also provides a time for educators to discuss student progress and concerns and to collectively generate ways to teach, support, and challenge all learners through the use of the structures.

Getting Started: Tips for Implementing the Structures

Begin using these structures in your unit or lesson planning with particular students in mind. Effective differentiation occurs when we consider our learners and find out about their abilities, preferences, and areas of intelligence as a starting point in instructional design. Then, look for structures that will allow you to teach the content you have identified while you address student needs, teach skills you want to foster, and potentially provide opportunities to address social and academic goals that are a part of a learner's individualized education plan (IEP). For example, if a student with learning disabilities needs multiple trials to retain information and also has an IEP goal to paraphrase key concepts from texts, *Popcorn* (p. 107) might be chosen as a review strategy for the entire class. This structure allows students to summarize learning in their own words and then teach or share the same content several times to various partners. By using this structure, the teaching team can provide avenues for the student with learning disabilities to work on critical goals identified by his or her educational team.

Keep in mind that all of the structures can be used individually, or they can be "stacked" to create new and different classroom experiences. For instance, a teacher might use *Popcorn* to get students talking about content and follow that activity with *The Whip* (p. 162) to find out one thing that each student learned from his or her classmates during the interview process. Or *Take My Perspective, Please!* (p. 168) could be used to elicit opinions or impressions about a topic, and it could be followed with *Stand & Deliver* (p. 154) to allow students to share one thing they learned from their interactions.

These structures are not subject or grade-level specific. We offer examples with each structure; however, if the example does not mirror your exact teaching experience, we encourage you to be inventive. The structures can be used in different ways across subject areas and with students of different ages, so they should definitely be edited, changed, and modified to fit not only your grade level but also your unique group of students.

Our suggestions throughout this book for adapting and otherwise altering the activities are not comprehensive; we intend these ideas simply to serve as examples of how certain activities might be changed for various types of learners and, perhaps more important, to suggest that they should be changed! In other words, we hope to communicate that adaptation, differentiation, and personalization of lessons for all students is what good teachers do. Furthermore, we are striving to demonstrate that when we expand or alter an activity to meet the needs of a single learner or a small group of learners, the result is almost always a lesson that is more comprehensive, responsive, and appropriate—for all. In Table 0.1, we have provided a short list of simple and quick ways to differentiate or design more universal learning experiences when using active and collaborative learning structures. More extensive ideas are offered in the section of each structure titled "Methods to Maximize Engagement and Participation."

To further increase your chances of meeting the needs of all learners, we recommend that you practice, practice, and practice. Avoid the common error of using these structures as beginning-of-the-year icebreakers—and only as beginning-of-the-year icebreakers. These structures, in most cases, are designed to be used as tools for delivering daily instruction, and with regular use, students will become more proficient and self-directed in their participation. So try a structure once, revise your plan, and try it again.

Keep in mind that during this process you may need to break down the structures into steps and spend some time teaching students *how* to participate in them. This may be particularly important for students with learning difficulties or those who struggle with change or novelty. Be explicit with directions, and be sure to teach both the rules and the social and communication requirements for working well in groups (e.g., sharing materials, paraphrasing a classmate's statement, expressing an opinion).

Further, you will want to explain to students why you are doing what you are doing and how it is relevant to the content. And always leave time at the end of an activity to debrief about what worked well or what might need to be changed to be more responsive to students' learning needs. You may even want students to reflect on the strategy so you can gather written feedback. Figure 0.1 is a student reflection form that can be used with learners in intermediate elementary grades to secondary settings. This same feedback can be solicited in a large-group feedback session or individual conferencing with younger children.

Figure 0.1 Student Reflection

Active and Collaborative Learning Structures

Name: _____

What structure did your teacher use?

_____

What content did he or she teach or review using the structure (e.g., fractions, Spanish vocabulary)?

_____

What did you like about using the structure? For example, was it fun, did you learn something new, or did it make learning easier?

_____

_____

_____

What was difficult or challenging about using the structure?

_____

_____

_____

What did you learn from participating in the structure? Be as specific as you can.

_____

_____

_____

_____

Would you want your teacher to use this structure again? Why or why not?

_____

_____

_____

_____

_____

Students may—at first—resist participating in active and collaborative structures, particularly if they have not had opportunities to do so in the past; this is a natural part of the learning process. Once they are familiar with several strategies we encourage you, whenever possible, to enlist their input in selecting methods to incorporate into upcoming lessons. Doing so will likely increase your students' sense of agency in their own learning and willingness to engage in the structures.

Finally, be sure to enjoy the process of this new and more joyful way of doing business in the classroom.

Table 0.1 Using Active and Collaborative Learning: Quick and Easy Ways to Differentiate and Design Lessons for All
• Have students work in pairs or in small groups.
• Bring therapists, paraprofessionals, other teachers, or volunteers into the classroom to help facilitate the activities and to give all students more adult support.
• Give directions or review the content in advance (preteach).
• Teach the structure to students first with less complex, familiar, or low-stakes content so that they can focus on *how* to engage in the process before applying it with higher-stakes material.
• Allow all or some students to practice the activity in advance, or video record the structure so the learner can see and hear what is expected.
• Allow students to have cue cards and preview materials during activities. Or let them use their phones or tablets to access the material, visuals, or supports they need.
• Allow students to have different roles in the activities; if most students are talking in small groups, one or two students might document responses they hear or serve as facilitators of groups.
• Ask or allow all students to use alternative or augmentative communication (AAC); you might, for instance, give all students the option to either speak or write a response during a group-sharing activity.
• Give choices in the activity (e.g., let students switch partners or stay with the same partner).
• Provide "wait time" or "think time" to one or all students before expecting a response.
• Use more than one output strategy (e.g., use pictures as well as words) when giving directions or providing instruction.
• Ask students to help in preparing the lessons so they can take active roles in leading activities, generating questions or content, and even creating supports for one another.
• Offer a range of tools for writing and expression, including paper and pencil, laptops, and tablets.

Acknowledgments

Many people helped us in the conceptualization and completion of this manuscript, but before we thank those who made the writing of the book possible, we must share our gratitude for the students with disabilities and many other learners with unique learning styles who have helped us think critically about Universal Design of Learning, differentiating instruction, and adapting curriculum. Although we have both taught dozens of learners who have guided our thinking in this respect, we are especially indebted to Mattie, Mark, Sarah, Sherrie, Paul, Jason, Franklin, Joe, Andrew, and Bob.

We would also like to thank the schools that have welcomed us into their classrooms to teach and be taught. Many educators field tested these strategies with us and fearlessly entered into an exploration of their own practice with students and colleagues alike. We are especially grateful to the staff members and administrators from Chicago Public Schools; Greenwich Public Schools in Greenwich, Connecticut; Madison Metropolitan School District in Madison, Wisconsin; Highland Park High School in Highland Park, Illinois; Deerfield High School in Deerfield, Illinois; Middleton High School in Middleton, Wisconsin; Oconomowoc School District in Oconomowoc, Wisconsin; and Verona High School in Verona, Wisconsin. In particular, we want to acknowledge the creativity and innovation of Matthew Armfield and Dr. Jeff Hoyer, teachers who contributed several ideas to this text and inspire us with their creativity, and the staffs of the Maryland Coalition for Inclusive Education (MCIE) and the Christopher and Susan Gust Foundation, who have used and promoted the book for years, given helpful feedback, and suggested helpful changes.

The work of many colleagues has shaped our thinking about curricular adaptations, differentiating instruction, active learning, and inclusive schooling, but we would like to acknowledge a few of them in particular. Dr. Lou Brown acted as our teacher and guide as we trained to be educators. He acknowledged and fostered our ability and desire to teach all children and to hold a steadfast vision of an inclusive society. He cultivated an urgent sense of advocacy in us to question the status quo, to reinvent conceptions of schooling, and to keep children with disabilities and their families at the center of decision-making.

Dr. Jacqueline Thousand and Dr. Richard Villa have been generous mentors in our professional lives. Their prolific work in the development of inclusive education provided not only the big ideas but also the practical steps to make change happen in complex systems. We thank them for inviting us along in the journey, sharing professional opportunities, and asking us to contribute our work to their publications early in our careers.

We extend extra-special gratitude to our friend and colleague, Patrick "Paco" Schwarz, who constantly inspires us to think differently, to innovate, to ask better questions, and to bring energy and fun to the classroom and into our lives. You are the best! You help us dream of possibilities!

The inspiration for the content of this book emanated from the ideas and the writings of Mel Silberman, Merrill Harmin, Jeanne Gibbs, Spencer Kagan, and Mara Sapon-Shevin. We are grateful for the work they have done that has made such a positive impact in the fields of teaching and learning, as well as in curriculum and instruction.

These acknowledgments would not be complete without mentioning the hard work and innovation of our undergraduate and graduate students from the University of Wisconsin–Madison and Syracuse University. So much of this material comes from our experiences teaching future educators; we are grateful to our students for field-testing these strategies in the college classroom, asking critical questions, and for working as change agents in public schools every day.

Our spouses and children supported our work on this project by allowing us to write, proofread, edit, and chat on the phone on evenings and weekends. Paula's daughters Erma and Willa were our resident experts on what is cool, what is interesting, and what helps kids learn in elementary and middle school. As Alice's daughters Madda and Haven moved on to high school and college, they have been able to share more critical opinions about what might or might not work in secondary settings.

Finally, we are grateful to those at Corwin for the time and care they invested in this project. In particular, we extend our very best to acquisitions editor Jessica Allan, senior associate editor Kimberly Greenberg, editorial assistant Katie Crilley, project editor Veronica Stapleton Hooper, copy editor Amy Hanquist Harris, cover designer Anupama Krishnan, and marketing manager Charline Maher.

Publisher's Acknowledgments

Corwin gratefully acknowledges the contributions of the following reviewers:

Joel Amidon

Assistant Professor

University of Mississippi, Department of Teacher Education

University, Mississippi

Sarah L. Schlessinger

Assistant Professor of Adolescent Inclusive Education

Long Island University–Brooklyn Campus

Brooklyn, New York

Melissa Sherfinski

Assistant Professor of Elementary and Early Childhood Education

West Virginia University

Morgantown, West Virginia

About the Authors

Dr. Alice Udvari-Solner is a national consultant in education and holds an appointment at the University of Wisconsin–Madison in the Department of Curriculum and Instruction where she has prepared preservice teachers to work in inclusive settings for over three decades. The graduate and undergraduate courses she teaches on the topic of accommodating diverse learners in general education settings are integral to the elementary, secondary, and special education teacher certification programs. Universal Design for Learning (UDL), differentiation, assistive technologies, collaborative teamwork among educators and paraprofessionals, and systems change toward inclusive education are areas that are central to her research and teaching. Dr. Udvari-Solner's research has focused on the development of the Universal Design Process for Differentiation—a method used to promote coplanning among educators to design responsive strategies for diverse learners. She has authored numerous journal articles, and her work has been featured in multiple texts that include *Leading Inclusive Schools, Educating Students With Severe and Multiple Disabilities: A Collaborative Approach, Creating the Inclusive School, Inclusive Urban High Schools, Quick Guides to Inclusion, Restructuring for Caring and Effective Education,* and *Creativity and Collaborative Learning.*

Dr. Paula Kluth is a consultant, author, advocate, and independent scholar who works with teachers and families to provide inclusive opportunities for students with disabilities and to create more responsive and engaging schooling experiences for all learners. Paula is a former special educator who has served as a classroom teacher and inclusion facilitator. She is the author or coauthor of more than 15 books, including *Universal Design Daily, 30 Days to the Co-Taught Classroom* (with Julie Causton), *From Text Maps to Memory Caps: 100 Ways to Differentiate Instruction in K–12 Inclusive Classrooms* (with Sheila Danaher), *"Don't We Already Do Inclusion?": 100 Ways*

to Improve Inclusive Schools, You're Welcome: 30 Innovative Ideas for the Inclusive Classroom (with Patrick Schwarz), and *"You're Going to Love This Kid": Teaching Students With Autism in Inclusive Classrooms.* To learn more about Paula, visit her personal website, www.paulakluth.com. You can also connect with her on social media, including on Facebook (www.facebook.com/paulakluth), Twitter (twitter.com/PaulaKluth), and Pinterest (www.pinterest.com/paulapin).

Introduction

Facilitating Inclusive Education Through Active and Collaborative Learning

During a visit to a parent advocacy group, we spoke with the mother of a young man with Down syndrome who was frustrated about her son's experience in middle school. Bryan, the young man, had been learning and fully participating in all aspects of classroom life at his inclusive middle school when the family moved across town to a different school that was also deemed inclusive. Before the move, the family was incredibly impressed with the education Bryan was receiving. His mother explained that Bryan was asking and answering questions during whole-class instruction, working effectively in cooperative groups, completing assigned projects, taking a leadership role in class meetings, entering the science fair annually, participating in school concerts and performances, and establishing positive social relationships with classmates without disabilities.

After the move, however, the young man's interest in school faded. The new school, although in the same district as the old and serving essentially the same population of learners, had a more traditional educational philosophy. Students were expected to sit in their desks for longer periods of time during large-group instruction and engage in more independent work. The principal explained that although the school was committed to inclusive education, they recommended it only for learners who "could handle it." In this school, he explained that learning "was taken seriously," and the teachers taught in more traditional ways to "cover all the material." Bryan began struggling, and before long, teachers were recommending that he be pulled out of their classes. Bryan's attitude toward school changed, and for the first time ever, he started resisting doing his homework, getting up in the morning, and even going to school.

Unfortunately, the scenario described by this mother is all too common; under one set of circumstances, her son is learning, meeting individual goals, and being effectively included. Yet in another setting, he is seemingly unable to negotiate the general education curriculum and instruction. As researchers and teacher educators in the field of inclusive schooling, we have been interested in and concerned about why these discrepancies in outcomes for students occur between different classrooms. Over the course of our work with educators across the country, we have attempted to examine what conditions, practices, and approaches facilitate the effective inclusion of students with diverse learning needs (Causton, Udvari-Solner, & Richmond, 2016; Kasa-Hendrickson & Kluth, 2005; Kluth, 2003; Kluth, Straut, & Biklen, 2003; Udvari-Solner, 1993, 1995, 1996a, 1996b, 2003; Udvari-Solner, Ahlgren-Bouchard, & Harell, 2016; Udvari-Solner & Thousand, 1996; Udvari-Solner, Villa, & Thousand, 2002, 2005).

We have consistently observed that students struggle not because they cannot learn the content but because they cannot learn in the way they are being taught. Too often, we expect students to change or to leave our classrooms when they experience failure or are disengaged. More often, we should be examining the classroom itself, questioning our teaching approaches and curriculum, and evaluating all the ways we might support, engage, respond to, and challenge every student. In other words, we should be following the key principles that underlie inclusive education (Falvey & Givner, 2005; Falvey, Givner, Villa, & Thousand, 2017; Fisher & Roach, 1999; Fisher, Sax, & Pumpian, 1999; Jorgensen, 1998; Kluth, 2003; Sapon-Shevin, 2007; Thousand, Udvari-Solner, & Villa, 2017; Udvari-Solner et al., 2016; Udvari-Solner & Thousand, 1996; Villa & Thousand, 2005, 2017).

What Is Inclusive Schooling?

Udvari-Solner and Thousand (1996) defined *inclusive education* as "a value-based practice that attempts to bring all students, including those with disabilities, into full membership with their local school" (p. 230). Inclusive education complements other school reform efforts by calling for a critique of existing school, teaching, and classroom culture. Administrators, parents, and educators are encouraged to question and reinvent traditional teaching paradigms and replace them with practices that value and encourage every student as a participatory member of the classroom community (Udvari-Solner, 1997). This progressive educational movement has evolved over the course of over 40 years, and key principles or tenets are well established to guide its practice. Specifically, in inclusive schools, we should see separate or segregated settings for instruction of students with differences dismantled. We should also notice that support services are being brought to the general education classroom and support personnel are integral members of teaching teams in general education environments. Most important to daily classroom practice, in inclusive schools we should observe that curriculum and instruction are collaboratively and universally designed by special and general educators (and, when appropriate, therapists, English language (EL) teachers, facilitators of enrichment programs, and reading specialists) with the intent to support every learner in the classroom.

What Is Differentiated Instruction?

Scholars and practitioners have used many different terms to describe *differentiation,* or the design of curriculum, instruction, and assessment that meets the needs of diverse learners. In 1995, Udvari-Solner proposed a reflective decision-making model for rethinking classroom practices and creating what was then referred to as "curricular adaptations" to better accommodate all students. Oyler (2001) used the term *accessible instruction* to describe the use of democratic practices and the development of challenging learning experiences. During this same time period, Rose and Meyer (2002) were introducing educators to Universal Design for Learning, a model that focuses on three different aspects of lesson planning: methods of engagement, methods of action and expression, and methods of representation. Udvari-Solner and colleagues (2002, 2005) extended this thinking by proposing a framework for differentiation called the Universal Design Process, which requires advance decisions about the content, process, and products of learning so that flexible and multiple approaches for teaching and learning are incorporated at the onset of lesson design.

In the mid-1990s, Tomlinson (1995) was promoting similar ideas and methods in her seminal book *Differentiating Instruction in a Mixed-Ability Classroom*. It was this text that popularized the phrase *differentiated instruction,* and soon thereafter, researchers, educators, and school leaders began using this term as a catchall for methods that are designed to reach, teach, and challenge a wide range of learners. Specifically, Tomlinson (1995) defined differentiation in this way:

> At its most basic level, differentiating instruction means "shaking up" what goes on in the classroom so that students have multiple options for taking in information, making sense of ideas, and expressing what they learn. In other words, a differentiated classroom provides different avenues to acquiring content, processing or making sense of ideas, and to developing products. (p. 3)

We like Tomlinson's definition and feel it has moved educators beyond thinking about curricular change as something that happens only in relation to disability. This definition also demystified the idea of differentiation, making change less threatening and more "do-able" in classrooms. However, we have been inspired to expand on Tomlinson's (1995) definition of differentiation. Throughout our careers, we have asked educators to articulate the influences and philosophies that have guided their work in inclusive education (Kasa-Hendrickson & Kluth, 2005; Udvari-Solner, 1996b; Udvari-Solner, 2003; Udvari-Solner & Keyes, 2000). When asked about their practices, teachers have provided a fairly complex and political picture of what it means to meet the needs of all learners. From those conversations, we have constructed this definition:

> Differentiation requires a desire to honor the individual. It is a conscious and critical act that calls into question what we teach, why we should teach it, and how we expect students to learn. Teachers attend not only to curriculum, instruction, and assessment but also to issues of relevance, meaning, and respect. A student's individual needs, experiences, and interests influence the design of learning experiences. The presence of difference in the classroom is not viewed as a liability but as the necessary catalyst for changes that will improve instruction for all.

Inherent in this definition and in Tomlinson's (1995) version is the need to look closely at and reconsider the process of teaching and learning. Specifically, we should attend to how we understand and respond to our learners and how students experience their education. Do they feel they are giving or only getting information? Do they have opportunities to demonstrate what they know and can do? Do they care about what they are learning? Are daily experiences fun or at least satisfying? These questions have caused us to turn our attention specifically to differentiating via collaborative and active learning.

Some form of active or collaborative learning is identified as a core tenet of most differentiation or curricular adaptation models. There are certainly many other methods used to differentiate that should be employed regularly, including using coteaching, arranging flexible grouping, developing multilevel and multisensory materials, making adjustments in expectations and goals, and employing student-specific teaching strategies (Udvari-Solner et al., 2016). However, we find that when teachers consciously engineer active and collaborative learning approaches, so many avenues to general education curriculum and instruction open that other supports, materials, and approaches are often unnecessary.

What Is Active Learning and Collaborative Learning?

Learning is not a spectator sport. Students do not learn much just by sitting in class listening to teachers, memorizing prepackaged assignments, and spitting out answers. They must talk about what they are learning, write about it, relate it to past experiences, apply it to their daily lives. They must make what they learn part of themselves.

(Chickering & Gamson, 1987, p. 4)

This quote by Chickering and Gamson captures the importance of making learning dynamic and interactive. Active and collaborative lesson formats offer alternatives to traditional teaching approaches that rely on whole-class and teacher-directed instruction. These strategies can profoundly and constructively affect the process of learning by offering multiple means to engage students and multiple methods for students to express what they know. Further, we believe that the use of active and collaborative approaches achieves positive outcomes by promoting student dignity and empowerment, facilitating self-management, attending to a sense of community, and increasing the energy and awareness of both teachers and students. These are outcomes we feel are essential to successful inclusive classrooms and that we are, therefore, trying to promote. In this book, we use the term *active and collaborative learning* to describe all of the featured structures because they incorporate elements of both types of instruction (active learning and collaborative learning).

Active Learning

Active learning involves putting students at the center of instruction and giving them opportunities to solve, explore, experiment, try, create, and invent. In classrooms that promote active learning, students are often moving, sharing, working in and out of their seats, using a range of materials, and engaging with others while talking or thinking aloud. Active learning is, essentially then, anything that students do in a classroom other than merely passively listening to the teacher's instruction. This includes everything from listening practices that help the students absorb what they hear to virtual learning via online field trips, Skype conversations, and Twitter interviews; from brief writing exercises in which students react to lecture material to short games used for review and introduction of content; and from complex group exercises in which students apply course material to authentic or real-life situations or past experiences (Paulson & Faust, 2010).

Collaborative Learning

Collaborative learning can be considered a subset within the category of active learning. Whereas many active strategies can be independently performed, all collaborative learning is inherently active because it requires individuals to interact in organized ways with others to problem solve, practice skills, or produce work together in some way (Keyser, 2000; Roschelle & Teasley, 1995; Udvari-Solner et al., 2016). It is a process by which students interact in pairs or groups with intent to solicit and respect the abilities and contributions of individual members. Typically, authority and responsibility are shared for group actions and outcomes (Panitz, 1997). Thereby, collaborative learning encompasses all group-based instructional methods in which students work together toward a common goal (Prince, 2004).

Collaborative learning changes the dynamics of the classroom by requiring discussion among learners. Students are encouraged to question the curriculum and attempt to create personal meaning before an adult interprets what is important to learn. Opportunities to organize, clarify, elaborate, or practice information are engineered, and listening, disagreeing, and expressing ideas are as important as the "right answers." Furthermore, in classrooms that encourage this type of ideology, the student is an active participant in learning rather than a passive recipient of education from an expert source.

Why Use Active and Collaborative Learning?

Historically, active learning and collaborative methods have been promoted and celebrated by a host of well-respected educators, including Socrates, Booker T. Washington, John Dewey, Paulo Freire, Maria Montessori, and more recently, Howard Gardner. Yet education in many American classrooms still tends to be primarily a passive venture. Students are often asked to sit in desks for long periods of time and learn through what Freire (1970) deemed "banking education." In this method, the teacher teaches and the students are taught, the teacher knows everything and the students know nothing, the teacher thinks and the students are thought about, the teacher talks and the students listen, the teacher chooses and the students comply, and the teacher is the subject of the learning process and the pupils are the objects (Freire, 1970).

Freire (1970) dismissed banking education as dehumanizing and called for a different kind of learning. He promoted instead a student-centered and relevant curriculum; a multicultural, democratic, and dynamic pedagogy; and a safe, tolerant, sensitive, and active learning environment. He felt that education should be pursued collaboratively, with student and teacher working in concert to teach and learn. Furthermore, he insisted that learners do not enter into the process of learning by memorizing facts, but by constructing their reality in engaging, dialoguing, and problem solving with others (Freire, 1970; Gadotti, 1994).

Understanding Theory

Freire (1970) believed in the power of active and collaborative learning and for good reason. Active and collaborative learning are firmly rooted in and draw support from a number of foundational social learning theories important to education (Udvari-Solner, 2012a, Udvari-Solner, 2012b). To illustrate, consider the theories at work when students engage in this example of *Classify, Categorize, and Organize* (found on page 86 of the book):

1. The teacher creates note cards, strips of paper, or pictures or provides actual items related to concepts that can be classified, categorized in two or more groups (e.g., different species of animals, parts of speech, types of architecture), or ordered into a sequence (e.g., numbers and mathematical operations that when combined make various equations and solutions, the phases of mitosis, the order of events in a story).

2. When the goal is to categorize information, each student receives one card or item that will fit into at least one category or group. Students must move around the room, viewing every class member's card or item to find others with related concepts.

3. When students believe they have correctly classified themselves, the group is given a short amount of time to determine the connections among the different pieces of information each person holds. Each group is asked to report its findings to the class. Group members may also add new or related information they know about the concept that is not represented on their cards.

4. The teacher listens to and observes the students' interactions while they are problem solving, assessing learners' background knowledge, conceptual understanding, and use of academic language. It is only after groups present their findings that the teacher provides input by asking questions, correcting misunderstandings, reinforcing ideas, or elaborating on key concepts. Watching students as they engage in this process can provide important assessment information about gaps in students' understandings or inform the teacher that students have a solid grasp on content and are ready for deeper or different applications.

This strategy was used in a fifth-grade integrated science and social studies unit on environmental citizenship to introduce key concepts and assess students' background knowledge. The general and special educator prepared a variety of pictures and actual items representing materials, products, or energy sources that could be sorted into the "three Rs" of environmental conservation—reduce, reuse, and recycle. The pictures or actual items included products such as paper, grocery bags, junk mail, cans, plastic bottles, paint containers, toys, Styrofoam, and energy sources (e.g., electricity, fossil fuel). First, the teachers simply asked the students to categorize themselves in any sensible way. Students logically grouped themselves by "like items" (i.e., paper products, items made of glass, and energy sources each clustered in separate groups). The teachers then asked students to reconfigure based on whether their item could be reduced, reused, or recycled, thus making the task more challenging because many items fit into more than one category. Students could deliberate until they felt satisfied with their sort and could justify their decisions.

Although the academic goal for most students was to compare and contrast the recyclable properties of various objects, Hayden, a student on the autism spectrum, had communication and literacy goals. Hayden was given a picture of a milk container paired with the word *milk*. His objective was to read the word *milk* and approach others to compare pictures or actual items to find a match. One classmate had the same image as Hayden, and another classmate had an actual milk carton. Based on similar materials, Hayden's classmates were actively seeking him out during the process of categorization to make comparisons, ask questions, and initiate interactions.

If we view this activity through a theoretical lens, we see these social learning principles in action.

Social Constructivism

A critical tenet of this theory is that knowledge or the way humans understand their experiences and reality is not simply constructed; it is coconstructed through the frameworks of language and culture in relationships among individuals (Palinscar, 1998). In this example, social discourse is not only encouraged but required to make meaning of the academic content. The individual must seek others to make deliberate comparisons, judgments, and analyses. In doing so, each interaction with another class member reveals new perceptions and interpretations, consequently shaping knowledge that has been developed collaboratively within a unique social context. In addition, learners have multiple opportunities to interact with and learn from more competent peers during the interchange of information, representing the zone of proximal development defined by Vygotsky (1978).

Social Learning Theory

Social learning theory emphasizes that by observing others and engaging in reciprocal social and academic interactions the individual develops new and more complex behavioral and intellectual repertoires (Bandura, 1977). The strategy *Classify, Categorize, and Organize* establishes an arena for individuals to observe the language and behavior of other group members while problem solving. Models are present as exemplars for appropriate attitudes, reactions to questions, and higher-level thinking skills. Since students must integrate their knowledge and information and then convey it to the rest of the participants, there is opportunity to rehearse or practice new behavior.

Social Interdependence Theory

Social interdependence exists when the outcomes of individuals are affected by the actions of others (Johnson & Johnson, 2005). The interactions that take place in the context of this collaborative learning strategy require and promote positive interdependence. To engage in the activity and ultimately be successful, students cannot function in isolation. By sharing their knowledge and finding relationships between what is represented on the cards, the individual is ultimately promoting the group's achievement of joint goals (i.e., to constitute a meaningful category that integrates each individual's contribution).

Social Justice Principles

In this example, students are placed in an empowering and "knowing" position at the outset of the learning experience. Rather than an instructor assuming the students are not knowledgeable and must be taught what is relevant, students individually and then collectively must use their existing knowledge to discover and make personal meaning from the content. They are not passive recipients of instruction that is dictated by others but have agency in their learning. The teaching/learning relationship is reoriented; it is a dialogue first among students and then with the teacher, who is informed by the students' discoveries of new patterns and conceptions. Students have an equitable role in conveying relevant concepts alongside the teacher. This process promotes greater spontaneity in instruction and ensures instructional time is not spent directly teaching what students already know or could discover.

Understanding Practice

Research at all levels of schooling has indicated that students learn and retain more when they have agency in the process and have opportunities to speak, listen, share, interact, reflect, and move. Much of the early research done on active and collaborative learning came from higher education as a result of concerns over learning outcomes when students were taught in traditional lecture-based paradigms. At times, we have been faced with resistance on the part of teachers, particularly at the high school level, who are concerned that it is counterproductive to use active and collaborative strategies because these approaches will not prepare their students for expectations in higher education. The following sample of studies indicates just the opposite—what we have learned in higher education in this arena must inform our work at every other level of education.

In a well-known active learning study, Ruhl, Hughes, and Schloss (1987) set out to explore what happens when students are given regular opportunities to make meaning of classroom content. In the study, two groups of university students received the same instruction in two different ways. In the experimental group, an instructor paused for two minutes on three occasions (intervals between pauses were approximately 15 minutes) during each of five lectures. During the pauses, while students worked in pairs to discuss and rework their notes, no interaction occurred between instructor and students. At the end of each lecture, students were given three minutes to write down everything they could remember from the lesson. Then, 12 days after the last lecture, students were also given a multiple-choice test to measure long-term retention. A control group received the same lectures as those in the "pause-procedure" group, but was given no opportunity to pause or confer with peers during the lessons and was similarly tested. In two separate courses repeated over two semesters, the results were consistent and telling: Students who experienced more interaction and were more involved in the learning process did significantly better on the daily assessments and on the final multiple-choice test. In fact, the magnitude of the difference in mean scores between the two groups was large enough to make a difference of two letter grades. This study suggests, therefore, that if teachers talk less (even *six minutes* less as in the aforementioned study) students can learn *more!* This finding is counterintuitive, as many teachers have been led to believe that student learning is boosted when more material is covered, not less.

Another study that challenges a common misconception in teaching was conducted with medical school professors. The instructors prepared three different lectures on the same subject; one lecture was considered "high-density," another was considered "medium-density," and the third was considered "low-density" (Russell, Hendricson, & Herbert, 1984). Ninety percent of the sentences in the high-density lecture represented new information, 70 percent of the sentences in the medium-density lecture represented new information, and 50 percent of the low-density lecture represented new information. During the pieces of the lecture when new material was not being presented, the instructor reinforced lesson objectives by repeating important ideas, highlighting the significance of the material, providing examples related to the content, and relating the lesson to the students' lives and experiences. Across the course of the study, students were given (a) a pretest (that showed no significant difference in their knowledge base), (b) a posttest immediately after the lecture, and (c) an unannounced posttest 15 days later.

Statistical results clearly showed that students in this study learned and retained lecture information better when the density of new material was low. The implication is that the amount of new information that students can learn in a given time is limited and that we defeat our purposes when we exceed that limit. In other words, teachers would be better off presenting only a few significant pieces of information and spending the rest of their time engaged in activities designed to reinforce the material in students' minds.

So in addition to teaching in segments, allowing for processing, and chunking material, do other factors impact learning in higher education? The answer is a resounding "yes." Collaboration appears to be key. In a highly regarded study funded by the National Science Foundation, Springer, Stanne, and Donovan (1999) reviewed hundreds of studies to conduct a meta-analysis of the effects of collaborative instruction on student outcomes in university-level science, technology, engineering, and mathematics (STEM) classes. A catalyst for this study was a report by the American Association for the Advancement of Science (1989), advising that the work of professionals in the sciences is not done in isolation, but that collaboration is necessary at all levels. Instructional methods that focused on traditional lecture-based teaching raised concerns that professionals would be ill prepared to solve real-world problems in cooperative ways. Frequent collaborative group activity in the classroom was called for at a national level. The meta-analysis conducted by Springer and colleagues showed that small-group learning for undergraduates in STEM classes had significant and positive effects on *achievement and persistence in courses* and that *students had more favorable attitudes toward courses* when compared to those who did not work collaboratively. Achievement variables, which included grades and test scores, suggest that changes in instruction have the potential to move a student from the 50th percentile to the 70th percentile in a course. In the area of persistence, classes using small-group and collaborative learning methods reduced attrition by 22 percent. Student attitudes about their own competence and the subject matter were also positively affected by their exposure to small-group instruction. Essentially, students liked their courses more, thereby maintaining attendance and their commitment to learning.

Finally, in the largest and most comprehensive meta-analysis of undergraduate STEM education published to date, Freeman and colleagues (2014) set out to test the hypothesis that lecturing maximizes learning and course performance by analyzing 225 studies. The findings documented that active learning led to increases in examination performance that raised average grades by half a letter (i.e., moving from a B to an A/B). Furthermore, failure rates under traditional lecturing increased by 55 percent over the rates observed for active learning. This analysis supports the theory that gaining and keeping greater numbers of students receiving STEM degrees could be achieved, in part, by abandoning traditional lecturing in favor of active learning.

These four studies indicate that teachers are working against lesson objectives when they resist methods that are student centered and responsive. More than one teacher has told us that he or she doesn't have time for active learning because of the standards or the amount of content that must be covered. The truth for these teachers is that they can't afford not to use active learning in their teaching if they want students to learn, remember, and use an ever-increasing number of facts, figures, ideas, and concepts.

Even the best and most entertaining lecturers begin to lose the attention of the audience within 15 to 20 minutes. A well-known study of information retention illustrates this point. Hartley and Davies (1978) demonstrated that immediately after a lecture, students recalled about 70 percent of the content presented during the first 10 minutes and 20 percent of the content of the last 10 minutes. Brain research reinforces these findings, indicating that continuous, intense attention to external sources can be sustained for only 10 minutes or less (Jensen, 2005). To promote and focus attention, Willis (2007a) notes the importance of intentionally building *state changes* into instruction. A state change can be anything that brings about a change in a student's thoughts, feelings, or physiology. Neuroscience also tells us that regular mental and physical breaks lasting anywhere from five to 20 minutes multiple times a day are needed to keep the brain in a receptive state for learning (Howard, 1994; Ratey, 2008; Ratey & Loehr, 2011; Rossi & Nimmons, 1991). In other words, a great lecture isn't really great if learners aren't understanding it, can't stay engaged, or can't retain the content.

Putting It All Together

We believe the active and collaborative learning strategies presented in this book provide vehicles for teachers to build in processing time, learning breaks, and opportunities for learners to imprint or "mentally download" material. In addition, the use of the structures creates the social culture necessary for constructing new knowledge and skills that are critical to advance student learning.

Of course, more effective teaching and learning is not the only benefit of using active learning (although it is quite significant). Teachers profit in active and collaborative classrooms, too. Educators often complain (for good reason) that they do not have opportunities to observe their students, work with individuals, or listen to the everyday "buzz" of the classroom. In other words, teachers feel that they cannot engage in many of the activities that would benefit their teaching because they are too busy leading the group. When teachers use active and collaborative learning techniques, however, they have more opportunities to try new roles and take on new responsibilities. Teachers who no longer need to be the constant "sage on the stage" are free during active learning exercises to interact with students, ask and answer questions, teach mini-lessons to individuals or small groups, and even stand back and watch students to evaluate their learning.

Beyond the pedagogical benefits, active and collaborative learning make lessons much more enjoyable for both students and teachers. Educators have revealed that when students who are accustomed to active learning begin working in their groups or engaging in a familiar game or structure, the entire mood and feel of the classroom changes. The volume rises, students are talking, interactions that might not happen spontaneously occur, laughter is common, and everyone has an opportunity to contribute and to learn.

Our explicit goal for this text is that it is used to create more learning experiences such as the one described in the previous paragraph; we hope that these structures can help teachers better respond to *all* of their students and create more inclusive, supportive, inspired, and, of course, joyful classrooms.

Building Teams and Classroom Communities

1

That's the Story of My Life!

Although many celebrated figures have the unique (and probably transforming) opportunity to create and share their autobiographies, ordinary people typically do not have the chance to tell their life stories. We think they should! Therefore, this activity allows students to share some of their personal histories and to develop new connections with classmates.

Directions

- Initially, students will work individually. Ask each of them to take a piece of flip chart paper and fold it into quarters so it is shaped like a book.

- Then on the front cover of their creations, they should write the title of their stories. To add a bit of whimsy to this part of the activity, you might instruct them to choose the title of a popular novel, song, movie, or television program (e.g., *The Time of My Life*, *The Fast and Furious Life of George*, *Wendy's "Believe It or Not" Life Story*, *"Orange County Girl"*).

- On the inside of the front cover (page 2), have students create an index of their lives, including the following:

  o Date and place of birth
  o Family information (e.g., number of siblings, names of pets)
  o Favorite hobby, sport, or interest
  o Favorite quote, phrase, or joke
  o Most exciting moment
  o Thing that makes them unique

- On page 3, ask students to draw a picture of their perfect day.

- Finally, on the back cover of the book, have students draw a picture of their future (e.g., family, where they are living, what they are doing).

- When all books are complete, have each student tell his or her story using the book as a visual aid. Depending on the size of the class, you may want to have students share stories in small groups.

- If possible, leave the books in a central location for the day or for the week so classmates can learn more about one another.

Examples

- A high school French teacher asked second-year students to construct stories using only the vocabulary they had learned the previous year. Then, she asked them to read their stories to one another, again using only the French they had mastered to date. Thus, the exercise served not only as a community-building exercise but as a review of vocabulary and an opportunity to polish their conversational skills.

- One elementary school teacher used this structure as a getting-to-know-you exercise during a year when she was welcoming Beth, a student with multiple disabilities, into her classroom. When Beth's mother asked if she should come and explain her child's abilities, strengths, history, and special needs to the class, the teacher decided it would be nice for all students to learn this type of information about one another. She wanted to make sure that Beth and the other students understood that all learners in the classroom were unique and special.

  Students spent a day collecting information for their books; this collection process involved interviewing family and friends, gathering artifacts from home, and filling in a teacher-prepared questionnaire designed as a brainstorming tool. Then, they worked alone (or in pairs, if assistance was needed) to construct their books. The school social worker visited the class to help students express themselves and tell their stories.

  The speech and language therapist also visited during this time to teach Beth some new sign language vocabulary related to the book; she also helped Beth answer all the necessary questions by using both the new signs and some pictures other students found on Google Images. Students spent two language arts periods sharing their work and asking and answering questions about their personal stories. Their books were then displayed in the school library.

- A high school psychology teacher used *That's the Story of My Life!* to give students opportunities to share personal information and to reinforce concepts from his class. Students were asked to include the following pieces of information in their books:

  o Full name
  o Place of birth
  o Family information
  o Favorite hobby, sport, or interest
  o Favorite websites/blogs/apps
  o Theorist that most intrigued them (e.g., Freud, Piaget, Bandura)

  Students also had to include the results of a personality test the teacher had administered. They could choose to illustrate the results in some way or summarize them in narrative form. Finally, they took turns sharing their stories with assigned partners.

Methods to Maximize Engagement and Participation

- Tell or share the story of your own life; show students a sample storybook featuring your own family, interests, and dreams. If you are working with younger children and you are using this structure to teach about diversity, uniqueness, or community, you may even want to invite other adults into the classroom to read their stories so that learners can see and hear about differences related to gender, sexual identity, family structure, and cultural and ethnic background.

- This activity is ideal for students who are new immigrants or who are simply new to the school to reveal more about themselves, their families, and their culture. Consider allowing these learners to also bring an artifact or two from home to share as a way of extending their story and further illustrating their life experience. Bringing artifacts might also be helpful for students with more complex or significant disabilities who struggle to communicate.

- Some students may need different materials to create their books; if there are learners in the classroom with fine motor problems, rubber stamps, stickers, and pictures from magazines and Google Images can be provided for them to use in the construction of their stories. Alternatively, these learners may want to construct their stories using PowerPoint or a storytelling app such as Story-Kit by ICDL Foundation.

- You will want to consider how well students know each other when designing prompts; students who have been educated together for years will be familiar with basic information about one another (e.g., full name, family structure) and may be more interested in gathering information about their classmates that is slightly more in-depth, such as their most embarrassing moment, family traditions, or travel experiences.

IDEAS FOR USING THIS STRUCTURE ✏️

_____

_____

_____

_____

_____

_____

_____

_____

_____

_____

_____

_____

_____

_____

_____

_____

AFTER USING THIS STRUCTURE

Did students learn what I intended? Were all students engaged? What changes might be needed to maximize engagement and participation for specific students? How can other team members be involved in co-teaching or instructional support?

_____

_____

_____

_____

_____

_____

_____

_____

_____

_____

_____

_____

_____

_____

Slide Show

In decades past, slide shows were a way to bond and share experiences. Friends, family, and neighbors gathered around a big screen to view images of a vacation, party, or new baby. The group would "ooh" and "ahh" with every image, and stories would be shared throughout the viewing.

Students today have certainly not experienced the type of slide show we are describing. They are growing up in a world with images that are as easy to share as they are to capture. This does not mean, however, that the community-building experience of gathering around the slide show needs to go the way of the carousel slide projector. We recommend, in fact, that you bring *Slide Show* into your classroom and use it to encourage students to take snapshots to tell their own stories and create connections with peers.

Directions

- Using phones or tablets, have students walk around the classroom or the school, snapping photos of people, moments, and things that represent them. They can take photos of others, of themselves, or of objects in the environment. They can also set up shots to create an image (e.g., scribble a phrase on a whiteboard).

- Put no limit on the number of photos students can take.

- After a set period of time, ask students to come back and review the photos they snapped.

- Now, ask them to narrow their collections down to just five images that best represent who they are.

- Finally, have students share their slide shows with a partner or small group. Repeat this final step a few times so that every slide show is shared several times.

Examples

- A physical education teacher asked her middle school students to create slide shows of themselves as athletes. She encouraged them to think broadly and asked them to capture images of their healthy habits (e.g., drinking water, eating vegetables), active hobbies (e.g., skateboarding, dancing), recently-acquired skills (e.g., doing a back flip, serving a volleyball), and wellness-related achievements (e.g., trying out for a team, running a mile, meditating).

- An English teacher used *Slide Show* both as a getting-to-know-you activity and as a way to introduce autobiography. Students initially shared a handful of slides to introduce themselves to the teacher and their classmates, but over the course of the semester, they added and edited to images to create a 10-minute story of their lives.

Methods to Maximize Engagement and Participation

- Create your own slide show, or share other sample slide shows so that students have a few ideas for content and style before they begin working.

- Make the task more interesting or challenging for some by introducing students to new photo editing tools, techniques, and equipment. Introduce apps such as Enlight by Lightricks Ltd. and AfterFocus by Motion One. Better yet, collaborate with your art or technology teacher on a slide show exhibition and ask him or her to work with you to teach new skills.

- Add to the drama of the activity by setting up a few projectors in the classroom and allowing students to show their pictures on the big screen (or wall or bulletin board).

- Have students start the project by brainstorming. Ask them to think about or even jot down these things:
  - Likes
  - Interests
  - Personality quirks
  - Values
  - Beliefs

  Then, have them make a few notes about what types of images would capture some of these elements.

IDEAS FOR USING THIS STRUCTURE

AFTER USING THIS STRUCTURE

Did students learn what I intended? Were all students engaged? What changes might be needed to maximize engagement and participation for specific students? How can other team members be involved in co-teaching or instructional support?

Our Classroom—In the Moment

Mindfulness practices have gained increasing attention as a tool to advance social emotional learning in school settings (Flook, Goldberg, Pinger, & Davidson, 2015). In simple terms, *mindfulness* is bringing our attention to our thoughts and feelings in the present moment. Formal mindfulness programs have been established in many schools, and early research holds promise that teaching students these practices can improve their energy, self-awareness, and attentiveness, while helping them reduce stress, manage negative thoughts, and learn to view challenges as opportunities. In addition, many of these programs foster compassion, empathy, and respect among class members (Black & Fernando, 2013; Goodwin, 2015; Klatt, Harpster, Browne, White, & Case-Smith, 2013; Kuyken et al., 2013).

Rooted in the values and practices of mindfulness, *Our Classroom—In The Moment* aims to promote self-awareness, attentiveness to the immediate circumstances, and ultimately a deeper appreciation for the classroom community. It involves students using mindful labeling—the act of naming what one is observing, a foundational skill in mindful practices. Although students are doing this reflective activity individually, they are still very much actively engaged in assessing the "moment."

Directions

- Select a time in the instructional day to introduce, teach, and practice the steps in this activity when the classroom activity level is already relatively calm and relaxed.

- If you have not used mindful practices before, it is important to provide an explanation of mindfulness as part of the introduction to this activity. Keep it simple and straightforward, as in the following example:

  Today we are going to practice something called mindfulness. (Check to see if anyone already knows about or uses mindfulness and can explain it in her or his own words). Mindfulness means paying attention on purpose to what is happening right now in the present moment. This means we don't think about what happened in the past or what might happen in the future. Mindfulness can help us pay attention to and be aware of things around us, such as sights, sounds, and smells, as well as our own thoughts and feelings. Doing this can help us notice when we become frustrated, sad, or angry and then help us calm down. It can also make us aware of the good things happening around us and notice when we feel happy. Taking time to experience the present moment can help us be alert and focused in whatever we are doing. Let's try it together.

- Ask students to find a comfortable spot to sit. When teaching the process, some students might do better sitting on the floor, at a table, or in a chair away from their desk.

- Tell students that everyone will take three big "belly breaths" together to settle their bodies. Explain that a belly breath makes your stomach blow up like a balloon when you inhale and then flatten out when you exhale. Model the breathing technique.

- Guide the class to take three breaths together with their eyes closed.

- Tell students to open their eyes and think about what they notice. It can be something they see, hear, smell, or feel as a sensation or emotion. If it is something they notice in the classroom environment, ask them to just name it or give it a simple description (e.g., soft carpet, red water bottle, Julie's blue eyes). If it is a sensation, such as a physical feeling in the body, just name it (e.g., itchy nose, sore ankle). If it is an emotion, ask students to be aware of their thoughts and try to label the feeling with a single word (e.g., happy, sad, angry).

- Explain that whatever they notice, they should try to be accepting—that means not thinking about it as good or bad, right or wrong, important or not important. Acknowledge that this is the difficult part and that it will take practice to let things "just be" as they are.

- To end the activity, tell students to think of one thing in this moment that they appreciate about the classroom or the people around them.

- Allow students to share these appreciative thoughts with a partner or with the entire group.

Implementation Tip

This activity will be most successful as a complement to some basic mindfulness activities such as teaching students to be aware of their breathing, to quiet their bodies, and to be attentive listeners. Mindful Schools (www.mindfulschools.org) offers helpful introductory materials for those wanting to teach mindfulness in the classroom. Another excellent website is Mindful Teachers (www.mindfulteachers.org), which provides numerous teaching resources.

Examples

- An eighth-grade teacher incorporated *Our Classroom—In the Moment* as a regular feature of his class meeting with students at the end of each week. He gave students sticky notes on which to write their appreciations; these were then posted on a whiteboard where everyone could read them before leaving for the weekend.

- After teaching this process to the whole class, a fourth-grade teacher used it as a method to encourage reflection in the moment as her students worked in cooperative groups to solve challenging math problems. After 15 minutes of problem solving, she stopped student discussions and asked every group member to follow the protocol: take three deep breaths, observe the environment or their feelings, then share aloud what they appreciated in that moment about their teamwork. For students who frequently experienced stress or anxiety associated with mathematics, this activity provided a reminder to be aware of their own physical states, to use deep breathing (in a manner that did not make them stand out from others), and to formulate positive thoughts about their group.

Methods to Maximize Engagement and Participation

- Make a movie. Some students may not be able to envision what it means to be "in the moment" or may just be learning how to reflect on their own thinking. Creating a video of this mindfulness process might be helpful for these individuals. Any educator (e.g., social worker, teacher) could "act" in the video, or a few students can be taught the technique in advance and filmed engaging in the process. Since pieces of the process are silent, the actors might use a think-aloud strategy and talk through what they are observing, feeling, and noticing. Alternatively, cue cards or thought-bubble cut-outs could be used for this purpose. The whole class would undoubtedly benefit from watching such a demonstration. A few students might even use a video like this to guide themselves through the mindfulness steps during free time or at home.

- Younger students or students who have emerging language might focus on just one observation in the moment. Responses can be scaffolded by moving from more concrete observations to the more abstract ideas of feelings or emotions with each subsequent session.

- A student who is unable to speak but can eye gaze or point can be given more direct cues by a supportive peer or adult. For example, "What do you notice? Show me what you notice by looking at it." Provide two choices of picture symbols representing emotions/feelings and ask, "How do you feel right now?" Prompt the student to eye gaze or point to the card of choice.

- After everyone is familiar with the process, select specific students to guide the rest of the class in the protocol. Get their input about the time(s) of day to engage in it. This might be particularly helpful for students with emotional disabilities or mental health needs because they will have choices in determining when these "moments" will take place. Establishing a predictable schedule that they have helped create may reduce anxiety and circumvent potential episodes of challenging behavior.

IDEAS FOR USING THIS STRUCTURE

AFTER USING THIS STRUCTURE

Did students learn what I intended? Were all students engaged? What changes might be needed to maximize engagement and participation for specific students? How can other team members be involved in co-teaching or instructional support?

Group Résumé

Just as a résumé describes an individual's accomplishments, a *Group Résumé* (Silberman, 1996) highlights the accomplishments of a team. Asking students to create a collective profile is an entertaining and effective way to promote reflection and self-assessment. The group résumé is also a quick and easy team-building strategy; students not only find out about each other but perhaps also about themselves. This activity guides students to focus on the classroom as a teaching and learning community and helps all learners understand the resources they have in their classmates.

There are endless uses for *Group Résumé*. It can be general or focused on content (e.g., *The Catcher in the Rye* Club, the Timpani Three), and it can be used to start the year or to summarize learning at the end of a unit.

Directions

- Explain to students that the classroom includes students with many different talents, experiences, gifts, and interests.

- Divide students into small groups and give every team chart paper or newsprint and colored markers.

- Ask each group to prepare a collective résumé to advertise their accomplishments.

- Provide suggestions for categories they might include (e.g., talents, skills, interests, experiences).

- After giving the groups time to work on the project, invite them to present their résumés to the class.

- Keep the résumés hanging for the rest of the day (or week or year) so that others can see the knowledge and abilities represented in the class.

Example

- In a high school art class, the teacher asked students to summarize their end-of-the-year learning by creating group résumés (see Figure 1.1). Groups were instructed to focus, in particular, on what skills they had acquired during the year, what abilities they had gained, and what information they remembered from class discussions. One group of young women who developed an interest in Impressionist art during the year titled their résumé "Women Who Leave an Impression."

Methods to Maximize Engagement and Participation

- To be sure that all students participate, provide ideas on how to elicit information from peers. Show students how to informally interview one another and how to ask questions that will allow each group member to contribute something. For example, if a student claims she cannot think of anything to add, or if she does not have reliable expressive communication, the other team members might share their contributions first, give that student time to walk around the room and get ideas from other teams, or let her draw or sketch ideas instead of name them.

- In their small groups, have students generate a list of questions and formally interview each other before assembling the résumé.

- Allow groups to create a video or audio résumé using sites such as Prezi (www .prezi.com) or Haiku Deck (www.haikudeck.com).

- Allow students to page through job-hunting books or to surf the web for examples of résumés. This will give them ideas for categories and content.

Figure 1.1 *Group Résumé* Example

Women Who Leave an Impression

Krisi, Nancy, Jen, Kana, Kim, and Katia

Qualifications
- Familiar with Impressionism
- Can compare/contrast Impressionism, Realism, and Cubism
- Can compare the styles of Impressionist painters (especially Renoir, Monet, Manet, and Degas)
- Have read autobiographies of Cassatt and Cezanne
- Have toured two major art museums, including the Art Institute of Chicago
- Have successfully completed six high school art classes
- Knowledge of the following:
  o Watercolor painting
  o Sculpture (wood and clay)
  o Furniture painting
  o Collage
  o Origami
  o Print making

Other Skills
- Sign language
- Wood carving
- Spoken word poetry
- Word processing
- Making beaded jewelry
- Sewing and designing clothes
- Making and editing movies
- Vlogging
- Singing soundtracks from musicals (e.g., *Wicked, Hamilton*)

Hobbies and Interests
- Reading fan fiction, watching old movies, listening to music (especially movie soundtracks), going to Great America and other amusement parks, following design vlogs, and karate

IDEAS FOR USING THIS STRUCTURE ✏️

_____
_____
_____
_____
_____
_____
_____
_____
_____
_____
_____
_____
_____
_____
_____
_____
_____
_____

AFTER USING THIS STRUCTURE

Did students learn what I intended? Were all students engaged? What changes might be needed to maximize engagement and participation for specific students? How can other team members be involved in co-teaching or instructional support?

_____
_____
_____
_____
_____
_____
_____
_____
_____
_____
_____
_____
_____
_____
_____

What Is It?

Is a broom always a broom, or can it be a lightning rod, a wall thermometer, or a huge cold-front symbol on a weather map? Those questions and more can be answered during a game of *What Is It?*

This structure is similar to games played by improv groups and is, therefore, sure to bring a little comedy into your classroom. *What Is It?* inspires students to look a little differently at their notes and readings, think on their feet, and play with content. It will also, undoubtedly, make the material memorable.

This game can also help to build classroom community. It's fun, it inspires laughter, and it also provides opportunities for students to give and get support and to learn from one another.

Directions

- Begin by placing an object in front of the room and asking the group, "What is it?"

- Then, encourage students to come forward and transform the object into something related to class content. For example, if a science teacher introduces a volleyball as the *What Is It?* object, one student might suggest that it is the planet Mercury. Another may pretend the ball is an atom. A third may create a scene in which the ball represents a single drop of water.

- The actors can tell the others what they are doing and how they are using the object, or they can be more secretive about their performances and students can shout out guesses about what is happening in the scene.

- Remind the group that only one student should approach at a time to act out a scene.

- After each performance, give additional information about the scene and the subject matter to add to the learning experience. Alternatively, you could enter and extend the skit as a way to reinforce content and make the material memorable.

Example

- An American history teacher presented a roll of paper towels to his class and told students they would be playing *What Is It?* as a review game. The students were, therefore, charged with using the towels in ways that would help all of them recall the content studied during the Civil War unit. The teacher first gave the students a chance to page through their textbooks for ideas and to brainstorm in groups of three. Then, he called for volunteers. The first student came up, unrolled some of the toweling, and pretended to read the Emancipation Proclamation off the long "pages" of the roll. The next student put the towel roll on his head to represent Abe Lincoln's stovepipe hat and pretended to be visiting a camp to shake hands with soldiers in Antietam. The teacher followed the humorous portrayals of Lincoln with a summary of some of the former president's political beliefs.

Another Version of This Activity

Pair this game with a close reading activity to support students with literacy learning needs. In this version, you will have students collaboratively read a piece of text or chapter on the topic of study. Then, instead of transforming a single item, direct teams to scramble and search the room for objects that can be used to represent the important concepts, ideas, and vocabulary words featured in their reading selection.

Methods to Maximize Engagement and Participation

- Invite students to form small groups and, after a few moments of planning time, ask each group to come to the front of the room to act out a scene using the prop. This team approach will be particularly helpful if some students have communication challenges, motor difficulties, or struggles with mobility.

- Show the object and have students brainstorm ideas for transforming the object with partners before performing individually.

- Provide choices. Put a few objects out on a table and let performers choose the one they want to transform.

IDEAS FOR USING THIS STRUCTURE ✎

_____
_____
_____
_____
_____
_____
_____
_____
_____
_____
_____
_____
_____
_____
_____
_____
_____

AFTER USING THIS STRUCTURE

Did students learn what I intended? Were all students engaged? What changes might be needed to maximize engagement and participation for specific students? How can other team members be involved in co-teaching or instructional support?

_____
_____
_____
_____
_____
_____
_____
_____
_____
_____
_____
_____
_____
_____

We All Own the Problem

We All Own the Problem (Davidson & Schniedewind, 1998) is a group problem-solving process that enables individuals to consider real issues and understand the experiences of others. This structure helps teachers cultivate a sense of shared responsibility, and it promotes the development of constructive solutions to issues important to students, classroom or school problems, and even content-based questions and challenges.

Directions

- Provide students with a question, situation, or problem statement (e.g., "Describe a recent situation that made you feel excluded" or "When has it been most difficult for you to be your true self?").

- After students write their response to the question, situation, or problem statement, put them into small groups (or into a large group if time allows) and instruct them to fold their papers and place them in the center of the table. Papers can also be placed in a container if you want to provide a sense of anonymity.

- Tell students to draw a paper that is not his or her own, read it, and think about potential responses.

- Then, invite them to answer the questions; one at a time, they should read the problem they are holding, consider it as if it were their own, and spend one minute talking about how it could be addressed. Then, the discussion should be opened up to all group members for the purpose of generating new ideas.

- Finally, have participants discuss their feelings about the process, the ideas they found useful, thoughts on using the process in other settings, and other issues that could be discussed in future sessions.

Examples

- In one middle school, this structure was used by teachers, administrators, and guidance counselors to create a forum for students to bring forward personal experiences on the themes of school safety, harassment, fair discipline, and other related issues.

- This framework was used by a teaching team in seventh grade to bring together a thoughtful group of peers who were willing to problem solve issues related to the inclusion of fellow classmates. The teaching team generated real issues and had them prepared for students to randomly select; they included the following:

  o Angela wasn't included in the seventh-grade talent show. She didn't even know about it. Nobody thought she had a talent. How could we change this?
  o Sarah sits alone at a table at lunch with an aide. Other students avoid that table, and she seems kind of lonely. What can we do about this?

  After generating solutions, the teams of students were supported by the adults to act on their ideas.

Methods to Maximize Engagement and Participation

- This structure as designed requires students to provide spontaneous responses. Many students with learning disabilities have difficulty generating ideas on the spot. The timing and pacing of the activity, therefore, may need to be altered to maximize the participation of these students. For instance, the theme of the problem-solving session could be provided in advance, so students could record some thoughts on the issue or dictate them to a peer or adult in advance of the session.

- A student who may have trouble generating ideas for the problems could be assigned to select and read the issues, then pick a fellow classmate to respond to each problem. In this situation, literacy and communication goals become the central emphasis of the activity for this student.

- Assistive technology should also be considered to support student participation. For instance, a student with multiple disabilities may be unable to generate a question or solution but may be capable of using the camera app on a tablet to record short videos of classmates reading the questions and generating solutions. These solutions and subsequent discussions could then be made available to others in the classroom. The student could also participate by selecting questions for peers to answer. If the student does not have a communication system, questions could be presented on different sticky notes or they could be uploaded to a communication app such as iComm by Accolade Consulting. Still another option is the All-Turn-It Spinner (see Figure 1.2). Photos of all the students in the group can be placed on the template, and the student with disabilities can use a switch to spin the device, and, thereby select a student to read a question or provide a response.

Figure 1.2 All-Turn-It Spinner

Source: Image courtesy of AbleNet Inc.

IDEAS FOR USING THIS STRUCTURE ✏️

_____
_____
_____
_____
_____
_____
_____
_____
_____
_____
_____
_____
_____
_____
_____
_____

AFTER USING THIS STRUCTURE

Did students learn what I intended? Were all students engaged? What changes might be needed to maximize engagement and participation for specific students? How can other team members be involved in co-teaching or instructional support?

_____
_____
_____
_____
_____
_____
_____
_____
_____
_____
_____
_____
_____
_____
_____

Pass the Compliment

Even after being out of school for 10, 20, or even 50 years, most adults still remember being teased, ridiculed, or taunted as children or as teenagers. This experience (and low-level violence) is often viewed as a typical part of growing up. This is unfortunate because put-downs can have personal and academic implications. Students struggle to learn when they do not feel safe, and stress is a horrible state for learning (Jensen, 2009). Teachers, fortunately, have the power to create learning environments that are positive and welcoming. They can even inspire a different kind of name calling and labeling in the classroom using activities such as *Pass the Compliment* (Loomans & Kolberg, 1993).

Directions

- *Pass the Compliment* is like the old telephone game played at childhood parties. Ask students if they know the game; if some of them do, invite one or two individuals to briefly explain the structure. Then, tell the students that they will play a version of this game.

- Begin by instructing them all to think of a compliment they would like to pay to the person sitting directly behind them (or next to them or in front of them). The first person in the row begins the game by turning around and whispering a compliment to the second person in line ("I think you are creative"). The second person in line then turns to the third person in line and repeats the first compliment and adds one ("I think you are creative and funny"). The third person in line turns to the fourth person in line and shares the two compliments as well as a new one, and so on.

- When everyone in the row has received a compliment, call on those in the front to recite all of the compliments from the entire row ("I think you are creative, funny, independent, a good cartoonist, and gutsy").

- Ask students to talk to their row members to determine if the messages got through or if some of them were lost in the process.

Example

- A fourth-grade teacher ended Friday afternoons with this community-building exercise. Students would sit in small circles and pass compliments around the circle until everyone had given and received one compliment. Compliments related to appearance (e.g., "I like your hair") were forbidden, as were those that were too general (as determined by the small groups of students themselves). In addition, students were encouraged to use a compliment that was specific to that particular week (e.g., "Your oral report was really inventive—I loved it").

Another Version of This Activity

Pick one or two students at the end or beginning of the day or week and have five classmates give them a compliment. Compliments can be general, or teachers can ask students to focus on something specific. For instance, a middle school teacher might read a student's story and ask his or her classmates to provide five compliments related to the story, which might include the funny title, the surprise ending, the really suspenseful part on the staircase, the good use of adjectives, or the great detail in the description of the golf course.

Methods to Maximize Engagement and Participation

- Help all students learn what a compliment is, what it sounds like, and what a good compliment includes. Some learners simply do not have practice sharing this type of information. For extra practice, begin or end the day or the class period by asking students to give group compliments (e.g., "We created amazing poetry this week").

- Be conscious that compliments and compliment giving vary cross-culturally, as do norms of interaction. For example, in some cultures it is expected that the person receiving the compliment will deny it to show humility. Ask your students who are English learners (and their families) about the compliments they commonly use and how compliments are given and received. Use the expertise of your English learners to teach these expressions and practices. Collaborate with the EL teacher to honor the cross-cultural differences among students.

- Bring in the school psychologist or social worker to coteach this activity. Some students (particularly those on the autism spectrum or those with emotional struggles and certain learning disabilities) may be receiving counseling or support to enhance their social skills. Involving other professionals can help students understand that cooperation and collaboration are schoolwide issues.

- Encourage older students to practice compliment giving via social media. Gratitude-focused Twitter accounts have popped up at middle schools and high schools across the country (e.g., @FFX_Compliments, @romeocompliments). Students don't need access to a specific account to spread the love, of course, but you might suggest a hashtag (e.g., #EastHighpassthecompliment) to get things started.

- Create a "Thanks for the Compliment" poster or chart to hang in the classroom at all times. On this poster, list words and phrases that are often used in compliments (e.g., "You are really good at _____"; "You always have great ideas for _____"). Seeing this language will not only provide a visual support for those who struggle to think of ideas for meaningful compliments, but it may also help students with emotional struggles (and others) to remember to be positive, reflective, and kind.

IDEAS FOR USING THIS STRUCTURE ✎

_____
_____
_____
_____
_____
_____
_____
_____
_____
_____
_____
_____
_____
_____
_____
_____
_____

AFTER USING THIS STRUCTURE

Did students learn what I intended? Were all students engaged? What changes might be needed to maximize engagement and participation for specific students? How can other team members be involved in co-teaching or instructional support?

_____
_____
_____
_____
_____
_____
_____
_____
_____
_____
_____
_____
_____
_____
_____

Two Truths and a Lie

Two Truths and a Lie (Bennett, Rolheiser, & Stevahn, 1991; Sapon-Shevin, 2010) is entertaining and energizing and can be integrated into the classroom as a get-to-know-you activity, a collaboration exercise, a curriculum preview or review, or a content-immersion technique. To encourage conversations that may be in some way related to curriculum, teachers can ask students to focus on specific topics for the exercise. For instance, students can be asked to share two truths and a lie related to ancient Egypt, the ocean, percussion instruments, or triangles.

Directions

- Instruct students to jot down three statements about themselves. Two of them must be truths, and one of them must be a lie (see Figure 1.3 for a worksheet that can be given to each student in the classroom).

- Then, have learners get into pairs or into small groups, read their statements, and ask their classmates to guess which statements are lies and which are truths.

- If time permits, have students share short stories related to their truths and lies.

Examples

- A third-grade teacher who often had students in her classroom who were homeless and living in temporary housing used this exercise several times throughout the year to encourage students to share information about themselves and to learn about others in the classroom. She was always gaining and losing students as families moved in and out of local shelters, and she found that this activity gave all of her students opportunities to get to know each other better and provided new class members, in particular, with opportunities to share something positive and interesting about themselves even though they had missed the getting-to-know-you activities in September.

  This creative teacher also used the activity to challenge her students academically and socially. If her learners were reluctant to try something new or to take a risk, she would whisper and remind them that the new learning or opportunity could be listed as one of their new truths in *Two Truths and a Lie* if they went through with the task or challenge. For instance, when one of her students refused to try simple stunts on the balance beam in physical education, she reminded him that he could boast about being a gymnast if he took the risk on the beam. Another student was encouraged to enter a community art contest when the teacher reminded her that she could call herself a "local artist" in the next game of *Two Truths and a Lie* because her painting would be on display at a neighborhood coffee shop.

- A high school art teacher asked students to choose an American artist to study for an end-of-the-year project. To get started on the projects, she asked students to do a computer search of their artists and then write two truths and one lie about them. One student, Marc, was assigned Jackson Pollock and wrote that he was a major force in the abstract expressionist movement, his style of art is

---

Figure 1.3 *Two Truths and a Lie* **Worksheet**

©iStockphoto.com/
kennykiernan

Name _____

Two Truths and a Lie

Write one statement about yourself in each box. Two of the
statements should be true and one should be false.

1

2

3

---

known as cubism, and one of his influences was Diego Rivera. Then, in small groups, students played *Two Truths and a Lie,* and three of the students in Marc's group correctly indicated that Pollock was not a cubist. The teacher pointed out that the exercise not only got students to start their research immediately, but it also gave them some introduction to or review of artists they would not be studying in great detail.

Another Version of This Activity

Have students write three facts about themselves that they think others do not know or will not be able to guess. Then, put all of the slips in a hat and have students draw them out one by one and guess who wrote each fact. After a few guesses are made, have the author raise his or her hand or otherwise reveal himself or herself.

If students share just one or two facts, you can play this game in a whole-class format. If students share three or more facts, break the class into small groups.

Methods to Maximize Engagement and Participation

- If you use this activity several times during the year, students may enjoy trying different prompts. For instance, you might ask students to share one truth, one lie, and one wish.

- In some cases, it may help to give students time to brainstorm about their lives. Give them specific ideas to explore, such as "What are five things you have accomplished?" or "Name three of the riskiest things you have tried" or "What is one thing that makes your family unique?" This will give those who have difficulty thinking on their feet options for their three offerings.

- Due to communication challenges, memory issues, or other learning difficulties, some students may have a hard time coming up with three things to share. These students might be encouraged to work with family members to write their three statements, or they might complete the *Two Truths and a Lie* worksheet with a teacher or speech and language therapist who can help and potentially even give some instruction in determining the difference between truths and lies.

IDEAS FOR USING THIS STRUCTURE

_____
_____
_____
_____
_____
_____
_____
_____
_____
_____
_____
_____
_____
_____
_____
_____
_____

AFTER USING THIS STRUCTURE

Did students learn what I intended? Were all students engaged? What changes might be needed to maximize engagement and participation for specific students? How can other team members be involved in co-teaching or instructional support?

_____
_____
_____
_____
_____
_____
_____
_____
_____
_____
_____
_____
_____
_____
_____

It's a Small World

Students will most likely be familiar with the expression "It's a small world." In this activity, they will have an opportunity to see what a small world it is in their own classroom. This team-building exercise asks students to think about characteristics that make them unique and those that bind them to others in the class.

This structure is especially useful to use in schools that are working to introduce students with different experiences or backgrounds to one another. For instance, *It's a Small World* may be helpful to use when a school has recently welcomed new students due to boundary changes or school closings. It's also ideal for use in very diverse classrooms where students with and without disabilities and those from a range of ethnic, cultural, and religious backgrounds will be working, sharing, and learning together. Finally, this game might be helpful to use with students who have not previously worked together in the past, as it can help to build instant connections.

Directions

- To begin the activity, ask students to find a partner. With that partner, they should make a list of at least five things that they have in common with one another, such as these:
  - Their favorite dessert
  - The month of their birthdays
  - The number of siblings they have
  - The color of the socks they are wearing
  - Their favorite movie
  - A YouTube video they love

- Once the pairs have completed their first list, direct them to split up and wander around the room, looking for someone else who shares at least one list item with them. Students then sit down with this partner and generate five new items of commonality.

- Have students repeat this exercise once or twice. When they are finished working with a few partners, ask them to come back to their seats and discuss their learning from the exercise with these starter questions:
  - What did you learn about your classmates?
  - What did you learn about yourself?
  - What did you learn about our community?

Example

- A fourth-grade teacher used *It's a Small World* on the first day of school so that all of her students would learn more about one another. Although most of them had been educated together for at least three years by the time they arrived in her classroom, some of the students were completely new to the school because of the district's new plan to close down a special education building and move students with disabilities into the same school as their neighbors, siblings, and same-age peers. During the activity, many students who thought they knew each other realized there was a lot they didn't know

Figure 1.4 *It's a Small World* Idea-Generating Worksheet

Name _____

It's a Small World

Fill in the blanks with a partner. You can write your answers or draw pictures to represent the answers, or you can both write the answers and draw pictures. When you have the same answer in one of the categories, put a checkmark (✓) in the right column.

Name: _____	Name: _____	✓ here if the answers match
favorite dessert	favorite dessert	
favorite color	favorite color	
type of shoe I'm wearing	type of shoe I'm wearing	
birthday month	birthday month	
favorite movie	favorite movie	
state I was born in	state I was born in	
number of siblings I have	number of siblings I have	
last book I read	last book I read	
middle name	middle name	
_____	_____	

about classmates they had been educated with for several years. Likewise, they learned they had a lot in common with the students with disabilities they were meeting for the first time. For instance, Richard, a boy with cerebral palsy, and his new classmate, Raul, realized that they both had spent time in a hospital (Raul for appendicitis and Richard for surgery on his back); both had three siblings; both had been born in Mexico; and both had the same favorite toy—the Xbox.

Methods to Maximize Engagement and Participation

- If some of the students are not familiar with the expression "It's a small world," explain to them that it is an expression used when you discover that someone you meet has similar experiences or has an unexpected connection to you. Ask certain students to share "small-world moments" they have experienced.

- Provide possible categories for students who might struggle to generate ideas on their own. Use Figure 1.4 or generate your own categories and share them with some or all of the students.

- Walk around the room and help pairs who are stuck; share new category ideas or prompt them to eavesdrop on other groups for help. Some students who have significant speech and language issues (especially those who have difficulties with pragmatics) may need the teacher to model the question-and-answer exchange that should occur between students to uncover similarities. For example, the teacher would lead the exchange by saying this: "Mindy, I noticed that you like horseback riding. Ask Julie in this way: 'Julie, I like to ride horses, do you?'" In addition, use your own knowledge of student experiences to ensure that learners are recalling shared events as a source of similarity. For example, you might recall aloud that six students in the classroom attended a school ski trip together.

IDEAS FOR USING THIS STRUCTURE

AFTER USING THIS STRUCTURE

Did students learn what I intended? Were all students engaged? What changes might be needed to maximize engagement and participation for specific students? How can other team members be involved in co-teaching or instructional support?

Makin' Mottos

What do you stand for? What is your story? What are your beliefs? Many groups—including corporations, nonprofit organizations, schools, and clubs—have mantras, themes, slogans, or mottos that bind members together and advertise or promote their common purpose. In *Makin' Mottos,* students learn about this process and create their own mottos as a way to build community and articulate a shared vision.

Directions

- Begin by asking students to discuss what a motto is and why groups or individuals use them (e.g., to promote unity, to promote the ideals of a group, to create a unique identity as a team).

- Then, put students into small groups and ask them to create mottos to represent their values, beliefs, or purposes in learning.

- To assist students in their brainstorming, share some mottos of well-known groups or companies, such as the following:
  - Girl Scouts: Be Prepared
  - Red Cross: Serve One Another
  - US Marines: Always Faithful
  - Little League: Character, Courage, and Loyalty
  - Nike: Just Do It
  - Apple: Think Different

- Provide time for small-group discussion and motto development. You can be specific about what the motto must represent or leave the task more open, depending on the goals or objectives of your lesson or of your classroom. You can even tie classroom content into this activity and charge students with creating a motto for a literary character or for a historical figure.

- When groups are finished working, invite them to present the mottos to the group.

- Finally, lead a discussion about the mottos and their meanings.

Implementation Tip

Because it will be fairly easy for students to come up with a motto in a short period of time, you may want to teach them how to brainstorm and require that they do so for a given period of time before selecting one idea from a list of suggestions. Remind students that "anything goes" in brainstorming and that the goal is to generate a long list (not the perfect answer) in this stage of the process.

Examples

- A seventh-grade social studies teacher used *Makin' Mottos* in the beginning of the year to help students come together as learning teams. He asked them to create mottos that would represent their views on learning history. Group creations ranged from the humorous "Learn It and You Might Win on a Game Show" to the more serious "History . . . Important to Look Back Before Moving Forward." He used the activity again to have students think critically about content. During a unit on World War II, he assigned a different country to each team and asked them to generate potential mottos for their nations. He asked students to come up with several options in a period of 30 minutes, and students then chose the one that best represented the essence of that country's struggle, attitude, and actions during the late 1930s and early 1940s. The team assigned the United States generated the motto "Making the World Safe for Democracy . . . Forever!"; the German team came up with the slogan "A Global Germany."

- During their unit on communities, a third-grade class generated mottos for their small cooperative groups. Then, they made posters featuring their mottos and hung them around the classroom. Tiala, a student with significant motor difficulties, could not contribute to the activity as her disabilities made drawing nearly impossible. Tiala's group therefore opted to create their poster online using PosterMyWall (www.postermywall.com). Changing the materials for this group allowed Tiala to select images, make decisions about the placement of those images, and work on her individual goals of independently turning on the computer, entering her password to sign in, and selecting a URL to get to a website.

Methods to Maximize Engagement and Participation

- As a way of preparing for the activity, ask students to make a list of ideas for which they personally stand or of their values and beliefs. If students seem to need assistance with this kind of abstract thinking or have never considered their strongly held beliefs, ask them to discuss the list at home. This way, students may gain not only ideas for their mottos but tap into funds of political, historical, and personal knowledge related to their families, communities, and cultural backgrounds (González, Moll, & Amanti, 2005).

- Let students do an Internet search for mottos so they get a sense of how different groups are able to communicate their values or mission in just a few words. You might encourage students to search for the mottos of their states, cities, or schools; religious, recreational, or political groups that are popular in their communities; or groups they care about personally (e.g., LGBT support groups, cultural organizations).

- Have students look up *motto* in the dictionary to get a more concrete sense of the word and concept.

IDEAS FOR USING THIS STRUCTURE

AFTER USING THIS STRUCTURE

Did students learn what I intended? Were all students engaged? What changes might be needed to maximize engagement and participation for specific students? How can other team members be involved in co-teaching or instructional support?

One Step Ahead

"I am a middle child." "I like zombie movies." "I have chocolate in my locker." Find out which students in your classroom agree or admit to these statements and others like them during a fun-filled game of *One Step Ahead*. This activity gives students a chance to compare likes, experiences, and beliefs and make connections with peers. In essence, this activity is a visual assessment of students and their attitudes, knowledge, or ideas. It is also a helpful way to get "all voices on the table" without requiring verbal communication. For this reason, this structure is an ideal icebreaker or review activity if one or more students in the classroom use alternatives to speech or have difficulties with on-the-spot verbal communication.

Directions

- Ask all members of the class to stand in a line at one end of the classroom.

- Make a statement about a belief, an idea, an attitude, or some piece of knowledge that learners may possess. Instruct students to move "one step ahead" if they can respond affirmatively to the statement or if it is true for or about them. For example, if the teacher says, "I am sixteen," then every student that age should move forward one step, and all of the slightly older or younger students should remain at "the starting line."

- Once all first moves have been made, make another statement. Again, have students move forward if the statement is true for or about them. Possible statements include the following:

  o I am the oldest child in my family.
  o I am 12 years old.
  o I have a pet.
  o I sing in the shower.
  o I am wearing blue jeans.
  o I am afraid of snakes.
  o I am a vegetarian.
  o I read *The Maze Runner*.

- Statements can also be related to class content, such as these:

  o I can name all of the planets.
  o My favorite character in *To Kill a Mockingbird* is Scout.
  o I was born in New York.
  o I can name a track-and-field event.
  o I know how to say *ocean* in French.

- When the first student or students cross the finish line, discuss some of the answers and responses to the statements.

Examples

- A math teacher used *One Step Ahead* to review for a semester exam. All prompts were related to class content:

  o I know the difference between a right angle and an acute angle.
  o I know the Pythagorean theorem.

- I can bisect an angle.
- I can define *ray*.
- I can find the area of a parallelogram.
- I know what *geometry* means.
- I can name a geometry-related career.

Throughout the activity, the teacher called on individual students to share their answers and to teach mini-lessons to the rest of the group. When only three students stepped forward and claimed to know the Pythagorean theorem, he called those three to the front of the room, had everyone sit down on the floor wherever they were on the "grid," and had the students reteach the concept at the board. Then, he asked everyone to stand and respond to the "I know the Pythagorean theorem" prompt again, waited for everyone to step forward, and resumed the game.

The prompts for the game were written by a fellow student who had been out of class for several weeks due to a serious illness. The student's first assignment on returning to the classroom was to review the chapters he had missed and develop some questions related to the unfamiliar content. In assigning this role, the teacher created a nonthreatening and enjoyable way for the learner to immerse himself back into his studies while giving him opportunities to get some support from his peers.

- An 11th-grade teacher used the article "White Privilege: Unpacking the Invisible Knapsack" by Peggy McIntosh (1990) to develop questions for this structure and as a method to raise awareness and open a conversation in her classroom about rising incidents of racism locally and nationally. Statements included these:

  - I can go shopping alone most of the time, pretty well assured that I will not be followed or closely watched by store employees because of my race.
  - At school, I can find many teachers who are my same race and have similar background experiences.
  - If I have an interaction with the police, I can be sure I haven't been singled out because of my race.
  - I can walk in my neighborhood at night and not be seen as suspicious or dangerous.

  Without saying a word, students were able to see who experienced advantages or disadvantages based on race and socioeconomic status.

Methods to Maximize Engagement and Participation

- List the statements on the board if some students need visual support. Or to get students involved before the activity begins, allow all students to list possible prompts on the board and choose from this list during the activity.
- Vary the prompts so that students with different types of knowledge and expertise have opportunities to share and move. For instance, you might have several prompts related to content (e.g., "I know the difference between ___ and ___"; "I can name three facts related to _____") and several others related to effort, attitude, or individualized goals (e.g., "I learned more than I thought I would"; "I met my individual goals for this unit"; "I could have worked harder yesterday").

- Give students a moment to "turn and talk" about the prompt with a partner near them before asking them to move. This way, students are able to ask and answer questions (this is particularly helpful if some learners are confused about a prompt) and give individual responses before engaging in the whole-class portion of the activity.

IDEAS FOR USING THIS STRUCTURE ✎

AFTER USING THIS STRUCTURE ✎

Did students learn what I intended? Were all students engaged? What changes might be needed to maximize engagement and participation for specific students? How can other team members be involved in co-teaching or instructional support?

Once Upon a Time

We have all heard the plea, "Tell me a story!" This activity is an answer to that request and a novel way for students to experiment with new concepts, ideas, and words. *Once Upon a Time* can serve as a brain break, a quirky review game, or a fun writing exercise. Use it to encourage creativity or to teach skills like sequencing, creating details, using descriptive language, and developing story openings and endings.

Directions

- Begin this activity by listing several categories on the board. For example, you might include
    - favorite book characters,
    - animals,
    - students in the class,
    - things you might get as a gift,
    - party games, and
    - common household chores.

- After generating the list, ask students to suggest items that would fit into the categories and write those responses on the board as well. For instance, in the "favorite book characters" category, students might name Katniss Everdeen (*Hunger Games*), Charlie Bucket (*Charlie and the Chocolate Factory*), and Hermoine Granger (*Harry Potter* series).

- Then, challenge the group to integrate those ideas or items into a story.

- Begin the story with, "Once upon a time . . ." and call on a student to fill in the next sentence. The object of the game is to incorporate as many of the items as possible from those generated in the classroom list. Therefore, a student drawing on the aforementioned categories might finish the teacher's sentence with "Katniss was playing pin the tail on the donkey when she noticed a mouse in the corner of the room."

- Inform students that they must contribute only one sentence at a time. Keep the story moving around the classroom until everyone has contributed at least one sentence. You can choose to end the story at that point or go around the classroom once or twice again.

Implementation Tip

Encourage students to resist overanalyzing their responses. Direct them to share whatever comes to mind. Remind them to encourage one another. This exercise should help students think flexibly and have fun.

Examples

- After teaching about avoiding colloquial language or trite expressions in their work, an expository writing teacher broke students into four small groups and told them they could invent a story about anything, but they had to incorporate at least a dozen trite expressions into the tale. She started the students out with this sentence: "I was working like a dog, feeling happy as a lark, when I saw John walking across the court, looking so angry there was fire in his eyes." Students recorded their stories using Voice Recorder by Tap Media Ltd., an app on their tablets. All recordings were played for the class at the end of the lesson.

- A fourth-grade teacher, interested to know what facts her students had picked up during their ongoing study of the United States, asked students to tell a collective story integrating

  o   a US river,
  o   a symbol of the United States (e.g., eagle, flag, Statue of Liberty),
  o   a state in the Midwest,
  o   a famous American landmark, and
  o   a US president.

  To add an extra level of challenge, some students with strong abilities in language and expression were told they would have to insert a simile, a metaphor, or an example of onomatopoeia as they took their turns in the exercise.

Another Version of This Activity

Use this strategy at the start of a unit as a pre-assessment and again at the end of the unit as a post-assessment of students' learning. Provide several categories related to important concepts, ideas, or academic language in the unit. Ask students to generate what they know in each category and then engage in *Once Upon a Time storytelling*. The story that is told may reveal students' background knowledge or misunderstandings about key concepts. At the end of the unit, ask students to add concepts, ideas, and academic language to the original categories and tell a story based on their new understandings.

Methods to Maximize Engagement and Participation

- Many cultures have a long tradition of passing stories down through the generations using storytelling. In some cases, master storytellers use gestures and vary their voice quality as a way of enhancing their stories. To interest kinesthetic learners, consider introducing gestures and other storytelling techniques and allowing students to use them as they engage in this activity.

- To make the activity more challenging for students needing enrichment, add requirements to the task, such as "By the end of the story, you must have . . ."

  o   included at least four vocabulary words from this unit;
  o   shared at least three learnings from the last chapter; and
  o   integrated three facts from yesterday's lecture.

- Use an app such as Shake-a-Phrase by Artgig Studio or a tool like Story Starters by Scholastic (www.scholastic.com/teachers/story-starters) to generate ideas for stories and provide a little extra excitement and motivation.

- Allow students, if necessary, to use alternative forms of communication to participate. For instance, some students may want to use some type of pantomime during their turn. Others may need to hold up picture cards that represent people, events, or ideas. If such an adaptation is necessary, have others in the group work together to interpret the idea and add it into the story.

- After generating the list of concepts, stop the activity momentarily and give all learners time to collect their thoughts and generate ideas. Some students may even need a "cheat sheet" with possible responses for each category listed.

- If one of the students in the classroom has intellectual disabilities or communication struggles, have this individual participate by choosing a story-starter card (e.g., "Once upon a time, there was troll who lived in a classroom . . .") from a group of three or more. Other cards could be used to inject a twist or plot change into the story (e.g., "And then something unexpected happened . . ."). The cards can be illustrated and constructed by other learners or by the teacher. Alternatively, the phrases can be programmed into a student's communication system.

IDEAS FOR USING THIS STRUCTURE

_____
_____
_____
_____
_____
_____
_____
_____
_____
_____
_____
_____
_____
_____
_____
_____
_____

AFTER USING THIS STRUCTURE

Did students learn what I intended? Were all students engaged? What changes might be needed to maximize engagement and participation for specific students? How can other team members be involved in co-teaching or instructional support?

_____
_____
_____
_____
_____
_____
_____
_____
_____
_____
_____
_____
_____
_____
_____
_____

Teaching and Learning 2

Wander to the Whiteboard

Want to hear from all of the students in your diverse classroom? Need a way to get them up, moving, thinking, and interacting? Just ask them to wander up to your whiteboard and show what they know. Let them think and learn, collaborate, and use images, words, and color to express themselves.

This activity is unique in that it turns the tables and lets students serve as teachers and allows teachers to learn from their students. This team brainstorming strategy can expand vocabulary, increase the use of academic language, and help students see how ideas are connected or expanded. *Wander to the Whiteboard* can be used as a review of concepts or as a strategy for checking students' prior knowledge.

Directions

- Give markers to a few students and ask them to write or draw something related to a topic or question you have placed on the whiteboard (e.g., "What is mythology?" or "What do you know about being an entrepreneur?").

- As students finish writing or drawing, direct them to pass their markers to someone who is seated. The person who receives the marker should then approach the board and add a word, phrase, or picture.

- Repeat this process until everyone has shared, or continue one or two rounds to let students make connections between ideas and add to their original contributions. You can specifically tell them what to add in each round (e.g., main concepts, a supporting element, an illustration), or allow them to make any contribution they feel is relevant or helpful.

- Finally, examine the board as a class and use the words, fragments, sentences, and images as discussion points or writing prompts.

Examples

- A second-grade teacher used this exercise to see student reflections on the question "What do you know about states of matter?" She labeled one of her three whiteboards *solid*, another *liquid*, and another *gas*. Students then came up individually and with partners to share short statements, such as "My backpack is a solid" and "A liquid can freeze into a solid like ice." Students also added quite a few images to the boards. The *solid* board included pictures of a baseball, a table, and a guitar. The *liquid* board featured orange juice, milk, and window-washing solution. On the *gas* board, students drew a balloon to represent helium and the sky to represent air.

- A seventh-grade science teacher with a number of students who were English learners in her classroom used this technique at least once a week to preview the concepts and associated academic language that would be used in the science text, lab discussions, and upcoming assignments. This created a supportive atmosphere in which all students were previewing and practicing new vocabulary words while making connections to their background knowledge. In a lesson on volcanoes, students were asked to consider how volcanic eruptions affect geologic landforms and people who live in the region. Students took turns adding facts, quotes from the textbook, key terms, and images to a huge sheet of paper taped to the wall. This diagram was then posted in the classroom so students could reference it and add to it during their unit of study.

Methods to Maximize Engagement and Participation

- Some students won't be able to write or draw to make a contribution. They may need preprinted index cards or sticky notes to affix to the board—for example, if the whiteboard work topic is *sources of light*, a student might be given single-word flashcards or pictures of the sun, a candle, a flashlight, the moon, car headlights, and a glowworm. This individual can work on choice making by selecting the cards to post or practice literacy skills by reading the choices that are given.

- A few of your students may want to have the role of facilitator. These learners can stay at the board and literally help to make connections between comments and images. Facilitators draw lines between points, observations, and phrases to create a mind map or word web. They can also encourage students who are reluctant to share.

- Include a wider range of students in the experience by widening your whiteboard. Cover your bulletin boards with chart paper, use easels to prop up poster boards, cover your floor with long sections of paper rolls, or let students make contributions using the interactive whiteboard. This way, most—if not all—of your students can be creating at the same time and choosing how they want to share.

- Have students work in small groups instead of as a whole class. Give every group the same topic or assign different-but-related topics to each group.

- When the group is stuck and unable to generate new vocabulary, terms, or ideas, assign a student or a few students to access an online visual thesaurus such as Visuwords (www.visuwords.com) or Thinkmap Visual Thesaurus (www.visualthesaurus.com) to search for additional relevant words and phrases.

- Assign one student as the "Whiteboard Wizard"; this student announces items the group must add to their whiteboard creation (e.g., a main concept, more supporting elements, additional images). Students who are augmentative communication users can act in this leadership role by having these cues recorded on their voice output devices.

- Try engaging in this collaborative process online using Popplet (www.popplet .com) or Google Draw.

IDEAS FOR USING THIS STRUCTURE

AFTER USING THIS STRUCTURE

Did students learn what I intended? Were all students engaged? What changes might be needed to maximize engagement and participation for specific students? How can other team members be involved in co-teaching or instructional support?

What in the World?

What can we learn from the world around us at any given moment? What do we lose if we stop paying attention to our natural surroundings? Peter Kahn, Jr., a psychology professor at the University of Washington–Seattle, has raised concern that the ubiquitous use of technologies puts future generations at risk of losing connection with nature and the positive psychological effects that are fostered by awareness and appreciation of our environments (Kahn & Hasbach, 2013). This strategy acknowledges the need to establish times in our instructional day to "get back to nature" for both wellness and academic purposes. Mini-expeditions not only serve as mental and physical breaks for students but may also ignite their interest in the natural world.

Directions

- Sanction some time within the day or week that requires students to observe or interact with the environment outside school walls. The key is to have a discrete and meaningful purpose for the exploration.

- Assign students individually or in small groups to collect data or information that can be used immediately or over time in their academic work.

- Engage in this structure for an entire class period or just a few minutes. Time allotments do not have to be lengthy—just enough to make an observation, collect an object, or even snap a picture.

Implementation Tip

When time or conditions do not allow for leaving the building, encourage short viewing breaks from a classroom window. Rename the strategy *A Room With a View* or something else that captures your students' attention. Place recording sheets, extra writing utensils, or recording devices at a permanent station near a window to be used in spontaneous moments or when students have unexpected free time.

Examples

- Students in a high school homeroom class were regularly invited to peek out their classroom windows and write nature-inspired poetry. Their arts-loving teacher suggested they draw inspiration from simple things like falling leaves, muddy puddles, and squirrels at play. She encouraged her students to engage in this type of small-moment narrative writing (Calkins & Oxenhorn, 2003) outside the classroom as well.

- A third-grade class photographed the same grove of trees all year long. One photo was taken each school day. The students compiled the photos as a video presentation to create a time-lapse record of the changing environment. This presentation was used to hone observational skills and teach about the effects of weather and sunlight on local flora and fauna. In coordination with the music teacher, the time-lapse montage was used as a backdrop to the end-of-year school concert to document and celebrate a year in the life of the school community.

- A fourth-grade math class drafted equations ranging from simple to complex while being outside during one class period. One student wrote a number sentence $(5 + 3 - 4 = X)$ after observing five birds on an electrical line that were joined by three more, only to have four fly away. Another student counted the number of pine needles on a portion of a branch, then attempted to estimate the number of pine needles on an entire branch and then the tree using the data sample. The next day students were put in small cooperative groups and given several problems from their classmates to solve.

- Taking photographs of the sun's position while logging the time of day complemented a sixth-grade lesson on Egypt and early inventions of timepieces.

- This technique was used by a ninth-grade biology class learning about symbiosis. Students were asked to find evidence of any of the five types of ecological relationships in their school outdoor space or neighborhood surroundings. Charts were provided to document evidence of competition, predation, commensalism, parasitism, and mutualism.

- In an urban high school, students were challenged to view their neighborhood from the classroom window and envision it with sustainable city concepts. Groups of students were assigned to design sustainable green spaces, locations for electric vehicles, bicycle routes, and passenger trams. Ideas for change were then presented to the city planning commission for future consideration.

- After providing an introductory mini-lecture about basic geometric shapes, a second-grade coteaching team had students explore the playground, school garden, and surrounding landscape to build geometric imagination and imagery. Some students were equipped with paper and pencil to sketch shapes. Others were given digital recorders to verbally describe their findings, while Eamen, a student with intellectual disabilities who used a wheelchair, was assigned to photograph scenes on a tablet.

Upon returning to the classroom, three learning stations were set up. The special educator conferenced with a small group to determine current understandings based on their observations and identified next levels of challenge with the material. A second station structured student partnerships to share, compare, and combine their findings. The third station was facilitated by the general education teacher and included Eamen in a central role. Using the pictures he had taken and a simple drawing-overlay program (e.g., Doodle Buddy by Dinopilot), each student outlined one shape found in the scene to create a nature scape analysis. See Figure 2.1 for an example of nature scape analysis using a photograph and drawing program.

Figure 2.1 Example of a Nature Scape Analysis

Methods to Maximize Engagement and Participation

- Consider how other types of technology and assistive technology can enhance a student's access and participation in the outdoor experience. Use digital recording devices for students to capture the sounds in the environment that may later help them describe their observations. For instance, the app MadPad by Smule allows users to turn everyday sights and sounds such as a passing car, the rumble of a commuter train, or the rustling of leaves into percussive recordings by capturing video and audio sound bytes. These sound and visual samples can be played in various combinations to make unique music compilations to complement student observations.

- Students who use augmentative communication devices might be provided prerecorded sentence starters (e.g., "I see . . ." or "I hear . . .") and digital photographs to help them capture thoughts and understandings.

- Students of varying abilities can be paired to combine their observations. One might take a photo while the partner generates a description. In small groups, specific roles could be assigned, such as the videographer, recorder, and data collector.

- Rather than the teacher dictating the focus of the expedition, ask students to generate lists of phenomena that interest them. Assign expert groups to periodically share observations and findings with the class.

- Use short visits into nature or extended views out the window as calming or self-regulatory strategies. Both the mental break and the "visit" with nature may be soothing for some students. In an interesting study conducted by Kahn and colleagues, a "technological nature window" was created by installing an HDTV camera on top of a building and then displaying real-time local nature views on large TV screen "windows" (Kahn, 2011). The researchers compared the physiological and psychological effects of experiencing the technological nature window to a real window view of the same scene. Findings regarding heart rate recovery from low-level stress indicated that *looking through the real glass window was likely more restorative than a technological nature view.* Kahn notes—and we agree—"Nature is good for us" (para. 4).

IDEAS FOR USING THIS STRUCTURE

AFTER USING THIS STRUCTURE

Did students learn what I intended? Were all students engaged? What changes might be needed to maximize engagement and participation for specific students? How can other team members be involved in co-teaching or instructional support?

Walk It to Know It

Although teachers routinely use bulletin boards, easels, and, of course, interactive white-boards for displaying important information, they often forget the untapped canvas of the classroom floor! The entrance of the classroom, the path from the door to students' desks, and even the tiles underneath these desks can feature images, words, or concepts that promote student learning. Teachers can use *Walk It to Know It* to teach any number of concepts, including the scientific method, binomial equations, or the parts of a business plan. This structure is especially helpful for visual and kinesthetic learners.

Directions

- To prepare for this structure, you will need to design flow charts (⇨☐ ⇨☐ ⇨☐ ⇨☐ ⇨☐) or series-of-events chains using one piece of paper or cardboard square for each piece of your chart or chain.

- Then, lay out your squares on the classroom floor in a pattern that will help you communicate the concept. If the content you are teaching is a chronology of events (such as the timeline of the Crusades), the pattern will likely be a straight line, but if the content is a cycle (such as the carbon cycle), the squares can be arranged in a circle or in any other shape that will help the learner understand and remember the material.

- As students enter the classroom each day or during a lesson when the concepts are introduced, have all of them stand and walk through the sequence.

- Have students explain each step as they walk over it, or simply have them read the information on the squares aloud. You might have students trod over the chart one time or several times over the period of a lesson day, week, or month.

Examples

- A fifth-grade teacher used *Walk It to Know It* to help her students remember significant events in the American civil rights movement. Every day when students came through the door, they were required to step on each one of the squares in sequence and read it aloud (see Figure 2.2).

- A health teacher used this technique to teach her students the steps used in CPR. The first day it was introduced, the entire class spent 20 minutes moving through the steps repeatedly. For the rest of the year, the teacher asked students to enter her classroom by stepping individually on each square. Furthermore, she assigned a short movement to each step of the process and occasionally asked students to step on the squares and act out each of the steps using the actions she had shared with them. For Step 1, which is to call out to the person, she had students wave their hands and yell, "Are you okay? Are you okay?" During class, she periodically quizzed students on the steps to ensure they were retaining the information.

Methods to Maximize Engagement and Participation

- Ask students to chant the words on each square as they step on them. This will help some learners retain the information more effectively.

Figure 2.2 *Walk It to Know It* Timeline Example

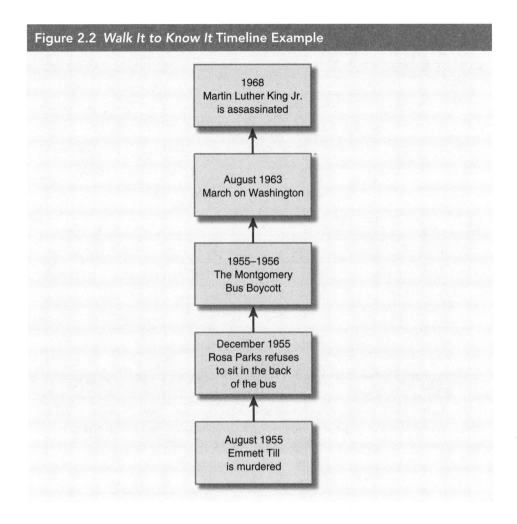

- Let students hop or skip through the sequence. Adding this extra bit of movement can give some students an opportunity to release energy in a constructive way. As in the CPR example, students might also be taught motions that relate to different steps and be asked to use these motions or engage in actions as they move through the sequence.

- To make the material more memorable, ask individual learners to help in the construction of the flow chart or event chain, or ask small groups of students to construct their own *Walk It to Know It* creations and have them take turns trying out all of the different versions. Students can print the text on the computer or write it by hand and embellish the squares with clip art, photographs, or drawings.

- Be sure every student can make their way through your chart or chain. If you have students who use wheelchairs or adaptive equipment in your classroom, be sure the entire *Walk It to Know It* sequence is barrier-free.

IDEAS FOR USING THIS STRUCTURE

AFTER USING THIS STRUCTURE

Did students learn what I intended? Were all students engaged? What changes might be needed to maximize engagement and participation for specific students? How can other team members be involved in co-teaching or instructional support?

Fishbowl Tag

Fishbowl (Silberman, 1996) is a discussion tool that brings students into a public forum to converse about topics of interest. In traditional formats of *Fishbowl,* students are gathered in two concentric circles. The inner circle is the discussion circle, and the outer circle is the listening circle. Usually, the teacher provides selected questions for the discussion circle to address. The listening circle offers observations and additional comments at the end of the inner circle's dialogue. After a period of time, the inner and outer circles change places.

Fishbowl Tag is traditional *Fishbowl* amplified! This version picks up the pace and transforms the process into a good-natured interchange of positions and ideas that will keep all students moving and thinking (see Figure 2.3).

Directions

- Arrange a small inner semicircle of five to eight students. Create a second concentric semicircle of the same number. The remaining students are audience members who look on and attentively listen from their seats.

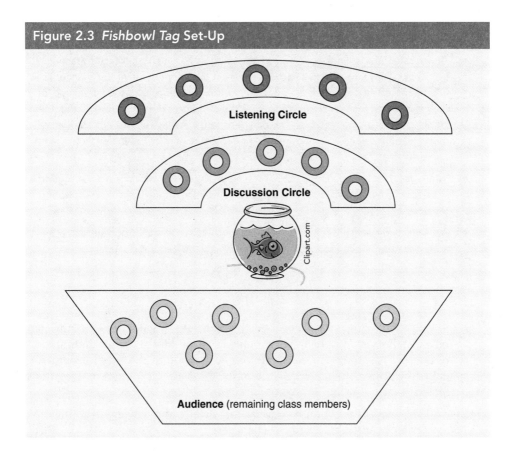

Figure 2.3 *Fishbowl Tag* **Set-Up**

Listening Circle

Discussion Circle

Clipart.com

Audience (remaining class members)

- Compose several open-ended questions or issues that will serve as a springboards for discussion. Toss the questions into a hat or—to extend the metaphor—a real fishbowl.

- Ask someone from the inner circle to draw and read a question. Then, let the inner circle respond spontaneously to the question, sharing knowledge and opinions. This is where the fun begins! Tell the inner-circle players that they may leave their chairs only after contributing an idea to the discussion. At that point, they can leave the inner circle and tag someone in the outer circle to replace them. The student leaving the inner circle then tags a student in the audience to fill the seat in the outer circle. The "tagger" then joins the audience.

- You can also allow inner-circle members to be replaced in another way. If they have already spoken in the inner circle, an observer from the outer circle who has an idea or thought to share can enter the inner circle and tag that member, thereby replacing them.

- Continue the discussion and game of tag for a designated amount of time.

- At the end of the discussion, note key summary points or ask for comments from the audience.

Implementation Tips

- At first, students will not be used to interacting with one another face to face in a semicircle. They will look to and want to direct their comments at the teacher for affirmation or next steps. It is important to define your role at the beginning of the process and even position yourself on the periphery of the fishbowl so that the students focus on one another. The only reason for the instructor to intercede is if misconceptions need to be addressed or if the dynamics of the dialogue become unproductive.

- When you plan to use this structure, set up "the fishbowl" in advance so that students can see the configuration and no instructional time is lost in transition to the activity.

- Ask for volunteers to be the first members of the inside circle, but thereafter set an expectation that all students will have an active role in the discussion.

Examples

- A high school English teacher used this structure to guide students through novel analysis. Questions were developed that prompted deeper examination of the text. All students were given time to respond to the questions individually in writing before being placed in the *Fishbowl Tag* formation. Questions included the following:

    o How does the author use organization, details, and imagery to define the narrator's attitude toward the characters?

- o   Consider the historical events in the text and the time period in which the book was written. What events taking place in the world at this time might be influencing the author?

- In a first-grade classroom, this structure was used as a forum for community problem solving when student disagreements erupted or when classroom relationships were stressed in some way. The prompts were based on specific issues that arose. For instance, when a question about lost items came up repeatedly, the group used this prompt in their *Fishbowl Tag* activity:

  - o   Some students have noticed that their belongings, snacks, or lunches have been missing. What can we do as a classroom community about this?

This same classroom teacher used this format to elicit comments about positive events in her students' lives and reinforce optimistic thinking through open-ended questions such as these:

- o   One thing I like about our classroom is . . .
- o   I hope that . . .
- o   One good thing that happened to me recently is . . .
- o   I'm grateful that . . .
- o   I wish . . .

Methods to Maximize Engagement and Participation

- Strategically select the most talkative students to begin in the outer circle; this will ensure that the game of tag will be advanced by those who have strong opinions.

- Let a student act as "tag master." This person does not have to enter the discussion circle but instead energizes and surprises the group (and usually inspires laughter) by tagging and replacing discussion members randomly. You might equip this person with a child's plastic fishing pole to "reel in" participants and add to the entertainment.

- To advance students' communication skills, the teacher can assess positive behaviors during *Fishbowl Tag*. Figure 2.4 is a rubric that outlines some of the behaviors that students should exhibit and also those from which they should refrain during *Fishbowl Tag*. To use the rubric, simply mark names or initials next to behaviors observed and provide feedback on these behaviors after the session. Middle and high school students can also be encouraged to use this form to observe and provide constructive feedback to their peers.

- To ensure attentive listening by the remaining class members (those acting as the audience), assign a critical observation task. See Figure 2.5 for a sample guided-notes outline that can be used to provide feedback to the discussants and debrief the overall experience.

- Some students may find the structure itself difficult to understand and learn. One way to ease anxiety and focus attention on the prompts is to ask all students to silently practice the movements related to the structure before giving them any content to discuss. Have learners walk through the tagging movements and the transitions between circles without having to participate in a real discussion.

- If some students on the outside need help to leap into the fray, act as coach by walking around the perimeter of the audience and (via whispers or sticky notes) giving students tips for making relevant contributions. You may even want to provide some students with cue cards that feature lesson-related facts or ideas so these individuals will have something appropriate and on target to share.

Figure 2.4 *Fishbowl Tag:* Score Sheet

Productive Discussion Actions	Student Initials	Less-Than-Productive Actions	Student Initials
Taking a position on a question; paying attention		Not paying attention	
Making a relevant comment		Making irrelevant comments	
Using evidence to support a position		Making points that are not supported with facts	
Leaving space for another person or bringing him or her into the discussion		Monopolizing the discussion	
Acknowledging another person's statement		Attacking someone personally	
Asking a clarifying question		Asking questions that are irrelevant to or disconnected from the discussion	
Moving the discussion along		Interrupting	

Figure 2.5 *Fishbowl Tag:* Notes and Questions

Name: _____

What did you hear in the discussion that was important?

_____
_____
_____
_____
_____

Did you have a point that didn't get presented? What was it?

_____
_____
_____
_____
_____

Who do you think was most convincing, or presented their point particularly well? What did they say or do that was convincing?

_____
_____
_____
_____
_____

What new questions were raised for you as you listened to the discussion?

_____
_____
_____
_____
_____

IDEAS FOR USING THIS STRUCTURE

AFTER USING THIS STRUCTURE

Did students learn what I intended? Were all students engaged? What changes might be needed to maximize engagement and participation for specific students? How can other team members be involved in co-teaching or instructional support?

Carousel

In this version of *Carousel,* colorful horses don't rotate, but a handful of "visitors" do! This structure is an entertaining way to have students generate and share information with one another. It also provides opportunities for them to present content, report on findings, or demonstrate skills without using a lot of class time. Perhaps most importantly, this activity shows students that they are experts; as students move from group to group and teach material to one another, the idea that knowledge resides within the learning community—and not just with the teacher—is continuously reinforced.

Directions

- Assign students to work in small groups. Then, assign each of the groups a number.

- Give the groups a task. You can give them a problem to solve, questions to answer, an issue to discuss, or a project to complete.

- After giving the students time to collaborate and complete the task, tell them they must assign one member of each group to be a visitor. This individual will leave the original group and present to other groups.

- Cue visitors to rotate based on their assigned numbers. Therefore, if the visitor is a member of Group 1, he or she moves to Group 2, and so on. The visitor from the group with the highest number initially moves to Group 1.

- When the visitors arrive, they share their original group's discussion, results, or outcomes.

- After giving the visitors several minutes to share this information, prompt them to rotate again. At this point, the lessons begin anew with the visitors sharing their original group's discussion, results, or outcomes once again.

- Keep the process going until all visitors have visited all groups.

Examples

- A high school drama teacher put students into groups of four and asked them to write a monologue titled "My Life," based on their experiences as teenagers. They had to keep in mind the elements of a powerful monologue they learned in class (e.g., personal emotion, having a point), and each person had to contribute at least three ideas. When students were finished writing, they selected one person to perform the monologue during a *Carousel*-style rotation. Each visitor, therefore, performed for each of the five groups in the class.

- A second-grade teacher used *Carousel* to give students practice in creating compound words. Each group was responsible for creating a poster of various compound words (e.g., swimsuit, lunchbox), complete with illustrations. The visitors then toured the different groups sharing their posters. Frieda, a child with cerebral palsy, had limited communication and was learning to use a new augmentative communication tool, the BIGmack switch (see Figure 2.6). She was, therefore, assigned to be a visitor so she could share her poster and have

Figure 2.6 BIGmack Switch

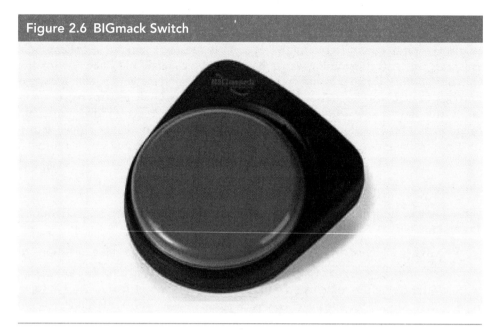

Source: Image courtesy of AbleNet Inc.

six opportunities to narrate it. At each station, she hit her switch to activate a 60-second message that explained the poster and was recorded by students in her small group.

Methods to Maximize Engagement and Participation

- Give students who benefit from repetition the job of visitor. If a learner is working on reading fluency, for instance, assign him or her the task of reading a poem, story, script, or list during the rotations.

- If a student identified as the visitor cannot easily summarize and share knowledge from his or her group, he or she might be given a graphic organizer or a cheat sheet of key points to use during the initial group's discussion and for each rotation.

- Have all of the visitors incorporate a product into their presentations. They might bring, for instance, a photo, drawing, infographic, or Animoto presentation (www.animoto.com) to illustrate or represent the work accomplished by their group; this product can enhance their presentations and make their teaching multisensory, which will in turn help the visual and hands-on learners in the groups.

- Use this activity to teach behaviors related to listening. Most of the students will not be in the role of visitor, and several may need support to successfully serve as audience members, so explicitly teach and assess skills such as focusing on the speaker, attending to support materials, and asking appropriate questions.

IDEAS FOR USING THIS STRUCTURE

_____
_____
_____
_____
_____
_____
_____
_____
_____
_____
_____
_____
_____
_____
_____
_____
_____
_____
_____

AFTER USING THIS STRUCTURE

Did students learn what I intended? Were all students engaged? What changes might be needed to maximize engagement and participation for specific students? How can other team members be involved in co-teaching or instructional support?

_____
_____
_____
_____
_____
_____
_____
_____
_____
_____
_____
_____
_____
_____
_____
_____

Novice or Veteran?

Use this structure when there is a clear discrepancy in the class between students who are more experienced and those who are less experienced with a topic or concept. In *Novice or Veteran?*, students who self-identify as novices on a topic have the opportunity to explore multisensory and multilevel materials to learn more about the topic, while students who identify as veterans on the topic formulate a fact or example to illustrate the concept. Members of the veteran group must then integrate their separate pieces of information into a coherent mini-lecture that is delivered to the rest of the class. For their part, novices generate questions from their individual study of the topic to ask (or stump!) the veterans.

Directions

- Share that every learner is both a novice and a veteran. Emphasize that the position of novice or veteran is dynamic and will change with different topics or skills—for example, it is possible to be a veteran regarding molecular biology but a novice in ballroom dancing.

- At the start of a new topic or unit of instruction, do an assessment or ask students to self-assess their level of knowledge or experience with the key concepts. Use the assessment to create two groups—one for novices and one for veterans.

- Give each veteran a single note card. Direct them to write down something they already know and can teach others about the topic.

- Give each novice a single note card. Direct them to write down one question on the topic. For this piece of the lesson, you will want to provide multilevel and multisensory materials to the group (e.g., photographs, videos, reference materials, different-leveled texts). Students can then use these materials to inspire their questions.

- During this time, have the veterans come together to share, validate, and integrate their separate pieces of information. The veterans' goal by the end of the class period is to mesh their individual pieces of knowledge into a mini-presentation for the rest of the class.

- Finally, have the novices ask their questions. Mark down any questions that stump the veterans as a priority for instruction during the unit.

Implementation Tip

To begin this activity, clearly explain the difference between a novice and a veteran. A veteran has past experience with the concept and feels he or she knows something on the topic that can be taught to others. A novice has less experience with the concept and would like to know more about the topic. It is important to emphasize that everyone will have the opportunity to be a novice or veteran at some point during the year. To reinforce this idea, you may want to intentionally put yourself in the position of a novice and have your students teach you a concept, skill, or process in which they have expertise (e.g., the use of a new video game or app).

Example

- In a second- and third-grade multiage classroom in which the teacher taught the same students for two years, the novice and veteran structure was used during a science unit on the life cycle and behavior of butterflies. The teacher of this classroom focused the unit on monarchs each year. The students who were currently third graders had experienced learning activities about this topic the previous year. By nature of the class structure, the third graders were veterans on the topic, whereas the second graders were novices. The teacher employed this structure at the start of the unit that focused on science standards related to the interdependence of life. A key objective was for students to understand that an organism's patterns of behavior are related to the nature of its environment.

  In this team-taught classroom, the special educator guided the third graders to recall their learning experiences from the year before, which included observing real caterpillars hatching into monarchs, releasing them, and communicating with children in Mexico (where the monarchs migrated). While the third graders prepared their presentation to explain these activities, the second graders reviewed written materials, photographs, and even models of a butterfly as they generated questions to ask their classmates. When the novice and veteran interchange occurred, questions that could not be answered were used as points of inquiry for the entire class.

  A second-grade student who was an English learner had moved from the Baja Peninsula and had lived in an area where monarchs gathered in migration. He was part of the veteran group due to his firsthand observations of the butterflies. In addition, any of the second graders who felt they had relevant "butterfly knowledge" could self-select as veterans.

Methods to Maximize Engagement and Participation

- It is important to use this technique across academic and nonacademic topics so that all students have the opportunity to share an area of expertise. Avoid having the same learners functioning as veterans or novices each time the activity is used.

- Some students may need support to build expertise or feel they have enough knowledge to act as a veteran. Providing some preteaching to particular students or giving them unique pieces of information to share can facilitate participation in the veteran group.

- Before the veterans present, have them review available materials to verify their perceived knowledge.

- Allow novices to work in partnerships or small groups to generate questions.

- For students who have difficulty coming up with questions, a list of them can be provided. The students can review and highlight the ones that are most interesting to them.

- Another role that might be used in this activity is that of moderator. This student could have the important role of logging all of the classroom questions and presenting them to the veterans. If the learner is an augmentative communication user, the questions could be entered into his or her communication system or uploaded into an app with a speech output function.

IDEAS FOR USING THIS STRUCTURE

AFTER USING THIS STRUCTURE

Did students learn what I intended? Were all students engaged? What changes might be needed to maximize engagement and participation for specific students? How can other team members be involved in co-teaching or instructional support?

The Walking Billboard

Too often in whole-class lesson formats, the same students raise their hands and share information day after day. This leaves many students, including those who are shy or not as confident in their responses, to participate only passively in these traditional structures. An alternative to calling on individual students to share responses to a single question is to ask all students to generate an answer and then to wear it around the room as a way of "advertising" their thoughts. *The Walking Billboard* will have them smiling, but it will also get them reading, sharing, connecting, and thinking about content.

This structure works best when you are seeking a variety of answers to a question that is open ended and has no clear right or wrong answer. You can use it for just a few minutes, or you can have your human billboards walk, show off, and share for an entire lesson.

Directions

- To begin, provide every participant with a sheet of flip-chart paper and a marker. Provide a question (or a few related questions) and ask all students to write or draw a response to that question on the chart paper.

- Hand out two pieces of masking tape to each student and instruct all learners to attach the chart paper to their clothing in some way; tell them they are now walking billboards.

- Direct them to wander around the room and read the responses on other billboards while being sure to give several different individuals a glimpse at their response. The other important direction in this exercise is that there should be no talking; *The Walking Billboard* is a quiet, visual activity designed to focus students' attention on what they see instead of on what they hear.

- Give students several minutes to wander; then, have them come back to their desks.

- Quiz them informally on what they saw and discuss their reactions to the assorted responses.

Examples

- An English teacher, teaching how to write a good short story, had students write responses to the prompt, "In a good short story, you will always find _____." Students then had five minutes to develop a response on a piece of chart paper. The teacher announced to the students, "I will know you are finished when you are wearing your response," and demonstrated how she wanted them to attach the paper to their clothing. When all of the students were wearing their individual responses, the teacher put a timer on for 10 minutes and instructed them to walk around the classroom and read their classmates' billboards. She encouraged them to view as many of the responses as possible without running, shoving, or disrupting others. When students returned to their desks, the teacher asked them to jot as many responses as they could recall on a sheet of paper. The class, as a whole, then discussed what makes a good short story.

- A high school physics teacher provided a mini-lecture on work and energy. She asked students to use a piece of notebook paper to write and illustrate as many featured key words and concepts as they could. At a stopping point, she had them wear their papers as billboards to view classmates' responses. This gave students a physical break and an opportunity to review content, but it also allowed the teacher to circulate and assess students' understanding of the material. After the exercise, the papers were collected and scanned as a collective document for the entire class to use for the next day's review and discussion.

Methods to Maximize Engagement and Participation

- Switch it up and let them chat a bit. During the sharing piece of the activity, you might opt to allow students to elaborate on their written responses and ask questions. This will help those who might not be able to get all the information they need from reading responses, and it offers support for students who are slow or emerging readers.

- To pique student interest, allow learners time to embellish their billboards. Some may want to add illustrations or stickers, use stencils, or write in an artistic font. You may even want to share advertising secrets with learners as they work to make their billboards memorable. For instance, you can encourage them to use bold lettering, develop catchy slogans, or create icons or images that their classmates will notice and be able to recall.

- Photograph students as they walk around the room; these images can then be used as a fun and informal review for those who want to revisit the content and the exercise.

- Have a student function as the researcher. He or she can walk around observing the billboards and record information on a chart or interactive whiteboard. This individual might also tabulate data in some way and report on the most common, most unique, or most notable responses via a diagram or list. This task might be appropriate for a learner needing enrichment or one who enjoys analytical tasks.

IDEAS FOR USING THIS STRUCTURE 🖊

_____
_____
_____
_____
_____
_____
_____
_____
_____
_____
_____
_____
_____
_____
_____
_____
_____

AFTER USING THIS STRUCTURE

Did students learn what I intended? Were all students engaged? What changes might be needed to maximize engagement and participation for specific students? How can other team members be involved in co-teaching or instructional support?

_____
_____
_____
_____
_____
_____
_____
_____
_____
_____
_____
_____
_____
_____

Dinner Party

At some point, we have all been to a dinner party where small clusters of people form and have brief conversations. As new partygoers arrive or people naturally mingle, the groups are reconstituted, and conversations are picked up or changed midstream. This learning structure mimics these informal group interactions but requires no cooking, no decorating, and no preparation!

Dinner Party encourages connection, collaboration, and communication. It can be used as team-building activity or as an alternative to small-group discussion and whole-class question-and-answer sessions.

Directions

- Devise a number of topics or content-related questions.

- Present the first question or topic and call a number between two and six. At this point, everyone is expected to stand, shuffle around the room, and cluster into groups based on the number you have called (e.g., if the number *two* is called, students would form partnerships). Students quickly share their ideas with the other members of their group.

- After a few moments, present a new topic or question and call a different number. Students must then switch groups and find new class members with whom to interact.

- After several rounds, ask students to share ideas that they heard in their small groups.

- Debrief with questions such as the following:
  - What was the most interesting thing you heard?
  - Did you find common themes in people's responses?
  - Identify one idea that challenged your thinking.
  - What is one thing you learned?

Implementation Tip

Provide more involved and complex questions for smaller groups (e.g., groups of two or three) and devise less complex (e.g., short answer) questions as the groups increase in size.

Examples

- In an introduction to a unit on probability and statistics, a teacher formulated the following questions for *Dinner Party* discussions:
  - What are some ways that data are collected?
  - Have you ever questioned the results of a poll or survey? Why or why not?
  - Share one way you have seen statistics used in everyday life.

  Students worked in larger groups to answer short-answer questions, such as "What are some ways data are collected?" and "Share one way you have seen statistics used in everyday life." They worked in smaller groups to discuss questions that required more discussion, such as "Have you ever questioned the results of a poll or survey? Why or why not?"

- A middle school instrumental music teacher used *Dinner Party* to help students teach and learn about jazz. He began by playing a piece of music by John Coltrane and asking students to form their first group. He then presented the following questions:

    o What do you hear?
    o What might the artist be communicating with this song?

    He gave the students a few moments to discuss, then had them switch groups. He put on a piece of music by Dizzy Gillespie and repeated the questions. During the course of a 50-minute class, he asked students to repeat this exercise using music from Billie Holiday, Etta James, and Thelonious Monk.

    Gabe, a student on the autism spectrum, was especially interested in this lesson, as jazz is his special interest area. To make this activity more meaningful for him, the teacher invited him to serve as the game's facilitator instead of as a participant. The teacher announced the questions, and Gabe announced the group size. He also was invited to provide additional information about the artists after students completed their *Dinner Party* discussions.

Methods to Maximize Engagement and Participation

- Some students (particularly those with language learning disabilities or those who are English learners) may find it difficult to respond to unexpected and fast-paced questions. Providing the questions ahead of time so that verbal or written answers can be formulated may be helpful. These answers can then be carried and used as a guide during the group discussions.

- The whole class may benefit from advanced review of the questions if they are unfamiliar with this learning structure. While the class is reviewing the questions silently, some students might rehearse their answers briefly with a teacher, therapist, or peer partner.

- If some students struggle to find partners during the transitions of the activity, you may want to facilitate some of the groupings by milling around the classroom and helping students assemble into the appropriate-sized constellations. To make even more purposeful partnerships, you can assign the groups in advance. Give each student a card that lists the name of each person to find for each new group. For instance, one student might have the following card cues:

    o Group 1—Find Tom, Amanda, Maia, and Kris
    o Group 2—Find Randy and Paul
    o Group 3—Find Ryan

- To make this activity even more whimsical, take the dinner party metaphor another step forward and serve punch or water and healthy snacks. These refreshments may wake up some of your sleepy students and literally give them "food for thought." Take it one step further and play soft music in the background as students chat and connect with one another.

IDEAS FOR USING THIS STRUCTURE ✏️

_____

_____

_____

_____

_____

_____

_____

_____

_____

_____

_____

_____

_____

_____

_____

AFTER USING THIS STRUCTURE

Did students learn what I intended? Were all students engaged? What changes might be needed to maximize engagement and participation for specific students? How can other team members be involved in co-teaching or instructional support?

_____

_____

_____

_____

_____

_____

_____

_____

_____

_____

_____

_____

_____

_____

The Company You Keep

Who shares my interests? Who thinks like I think? Who knows what I know? Students can find answers to these and other questions in this fast-paced game from Mel Silberman (1996). *The Company You Keep* is appropriate as a review, an icebreaker, or an introduction to new material. It can last for 30 minutes and be used to teach a lesson, or it can recap the day's learning during the last five minutes of a class period. This structure allows students to learn about the perspectives and knowledge of their classmates and gives participants opportunities to see interests, ideas, and even values they share with one another.

Directions

- To prepare for this game, make a list of questions that (a) are appropriate for teaching or reviewing content and (b) give students an opportunity to make a controlled choice. In other words, the questions should have limited answers. Examples include the following:
  - Do you agree or disagree with capital punishment?
  - Do you or do you not understand how to multiply binomials?
  - Who is your favorite character from *The Color Purple?*
  - What Spanish-speaking nation would you most like to visit?

- Then, clear some space in the classroom or move students to a hallway.

- Call out a question and ask students to mill around the classroom looking for all others who have the same answer they do. Therefore, students who agree with capital punishment would cluster together, and those who disagree would do the same. If the prompt contains multiple responses, the teacher should tell students to cluster together with their small group and to make sure they move away from other groups so all discrete groups can be identified.

- When students have formed groups, have them shake hands with the "company they keep." Then, do some debriefing with the class. You might ask students to discuss the category they chose or to explain why they chose what they did—for example, if you had students choose their favorite character from a book, you can call on individuals to defend their choices and invite students in other groups to interrogate these choices and ask clarifying questions.

Implementation Tip

You may want to ask students to sit down together or to link arms once groups have formed, so all participants can clearly see what groups are represented and where each one is located. For further clarification, students might even be asked to hold up signs indicating the name or identity of their group.

Examples

- When a fifth-grade class was studying regions (e.g., the Northwest, the Midwest) of the United States, the teacher asked them to respond to the following prompts and find the "company they keep":
  - o Region in which I was born
  - o Region I would most like to visit
  - o Region that has or appears to have the best tourist attractions
  - o Region that seems the most beautiful
  - o Region that seems to have the most important natural resources

  To prepare for this exercise, the teacher asked the students to review the information in their textbooks on these particular issues (e.g., natural resources, tourism) so they would be able to give thoughtful, evidence-based reasons for making choices.

- During a unit on *Of Mice and Men,* a high school English teacher asked students to find the "company they keep" for the following opinions:
  - o Character in the book they most respected
  - o Character in the book they felt was the most misunderstood
  - o Character in the book they felt was the weakest
  - o Character in the book they felt was the most sympathetic

  As students met with each new group, they discussed why they chose the character and what specific evidence from the book drove their decision. Students needing a bit more support in identifying and remembering character traits and motivations carried their tablets with them to check their notes when necessary or to peek at highlighted copies of the text on their e-readers.

Methods to Maximize Engagement and Participation

- Some students may need more information in order to make a choice—for example, if students are asked to identify the aerobic exercise they like the most, some may easily be able to find a group by looking for other runners or bikers, but some students may not know what aerobic exercise is or what types of activities fall into that category. Those learners will need some preteaching on this topic to generate a response.

- Show and tell. Write the prompts on the whiteboard so that students can both hear and see choices, or give certain students an index card with this information on it so they can have a reminder of the task and the prompts as they make their way around the room.

- Be quiet. To make the activity slightly more challenging (and to create built-in supports for English learners), ask the students to find "their company" without speaking. This way, students have to be very creative in locating others in their group.

- Once students are in their respective groups, call on individual students to defend or explain why they chose as they did. Vary questions to suit the needs and abilities of each student. You might ask very concrete questions of some learners (e.g., Why do you like George?) and very complex questions of other students (e.g., Who or what does George symbolize?).

IDEAS FOR USING THIS STRUCTURE

AFTER USING THIS STRUCTURE

Did students learn what I intended? Were all students engaged? What changes might be needed to maximize engagement and participation for specific students? How can other team members be involved in co-teaching or instructional support?

Classify, Categorize, and Organize

This structure promotes learning by discovery and problem solving by expecting students to make sense of new information and convey it to the class. It also helps students see the connections between separate pieces of information and take an active role in presenting key concepts alongside the teacher. Often when students are given the opportunity to grapple with content on their own, they will develop teaching points that the instructor had intended to provide. This process promotes greater spontaneity in instruction and ensures class time is not spent directly teaching what students already know or could be supported to discover.

Directions

- Create note cards, strips of paper, or actual pictures related to concepts that can be classified, categorized in two or more groups, or ordered (e.g., different species of animals, parts of speech).

- Give each student in the class one card (or paper slip or picture) that will fit into at least one category or group. Then, encourage students to move around the room, view each other's cards, and find those who belong in their group.

- When students finish the sort, give the group time to identify its category and determine how the different pieces of information are related. Each group should then be asked to report its observations and conclusions to the class. The group members may also add novel or additional information they know about the concept or topic that is not represented on their cards.

- After each group presents, use the information to reinforce important points, clear up misconceptions, or provide a short mini-lecture on the topic as a whole.

Implementation Tip

To simplify the task for your students and to save time, you can provide the categories to the class at the start of the activity (e.g., "You all have a country written on your card. You are looking for students with countries that are on the same continent as your country").

Examples

- A librarian at an elementary school used this technique to teach students about literary genres. She gave each student an actual book and asked them to look at the title and read the book description. Students had to group themselves by genres of their assigned book (e.g., mystery, suspense, horror, drama, science fiction).

- A first-grade teacher used this structure to teach animal classifications (e.g., birds, reptiles, mammals, amphibians, fish). For a student with Down syndrome and moderate intellectual disabilities, participation in this activity focused on language and reading goals. His primary objective was to identify the picture of a snake and read the words *scaly skin* from his card loudly enough to be heard by others in the class. Other students in the room had to determine whether this student's card fit into their category.

- A fourth-grade general and special educator teaching team created cards that constituted a number of different equations. When put together correctly, a solution was evident. Here is a sample of the cards developed: 2, 10, ($\times$), 15, 12, ($-$), 13, ($=$), 120, ($=$). When students correctly configured themselves in two groups of four, these equations were formed: $10 \times 12 = 120$ and $15 - 13 = 2$. The teachers could differentiate easily by creating cards (and ultimately equations) that ranged in difficulty level. Some student groups formed algebraic equations, others created fractions, and still others represented the process of addition or subtraction.

- In a high school health science class that was focusing on medical interventions, generic names of a wide range of pharmacological drugs were written on cards. In three rounds, students were asked to classify themselves in different ways: first, by drug type (e.g., stimulants, antidepressants, diuretics); second, by the side effects of the drug; and third, by the way it is used to treat a particular condition.

Methods to Maximize Engagement and Participation

- If a student does not yet have skills to accurately associate his or her card information to a category, directly teach him or her what information to look for— for example, "You have an owl on your card. An owl is a bird. You should look for other people who have birds on their cards." If even this is too complex, you could change the objective of the activity completely and ask the learner to simply find a match to his or her card. In this scenario, you would need two identical owl cards, and you would give the student the task of finding another owl; the two students would then need to find their *Classify, Categorize, and Organize* group together.

- Give one student the name of the unifying category on a separate colored card; others must come to him or her to form a logical group. This adaptation might be especially helpful for those needing extra support, as these students do not have the responsibility of finding a group; instead, students find them. These cards might also contain extra information about the topic or group (e.g., because an amphibian's skin lacks a shell, scales, or outer drier covering, most live in wet or damp areas to prevent dehydration) so that the student holding that card can share information (and serve in an expert role) with the group once it is assembled.

- Mix up the type of information given to different students. Some information on the cards may be in single words, others in short phrases, and still others in picture form.

- If you have a student who struggles with collaborative learning and may feel nervous about chatting with classmates, provide him or her with a card that contains content that he or she knows well and can potentially teach to others.

- For a student who is ready for more challenging decisions and interactions, prepare a card that can fit in multiple categories. The student with this card must justify his or her associations with several student groups.

IDEAS FOR USING THIS STRUCTURE ✎

_____
_____
_____
_____
_____
_____
_____
_____
_____
_____
_____
_____
_____
_____
_____

AFTER USING THIS STRUCTURE

Did students learn what I intended? Were all students engaged? What changes might be needed to maximize engagement and participation for specific students? How can other team members be involved in co-teaching or instructional support?

_____
_____
_____
_____
_____
_____
_____
_____
_____
_____
_____
_____
_____
_____

Collective Brainwriting

This technique illustrates the adage "Two heads are better than one." In *Collective Brainwriting*, students generate solutions to multiple issues posed at the same time in small problem-solving groups. Depending on the topics used, this strategy can be either high energy or relatively quiet and low-key and can, therefore, be adjusted to meet the needs of students and the requirements of the task.

Directions

- Place students in groups ranging in size from four to eight members. Direct each person in the group to think of an issue or problem to be solved and to summarize it in writing on a half-sheet of paper.

- When they are finished writing, tell students to place their papers in the middle of the table.

- Students should then be asked to take a paper that is not his or her own, read the problem silently, and write at least one idea on the bottom half of the paper.

- When students complete this step, ask them to return these papers to the center of the table and again choose a new one (or, alternatively, pass their papers to the left). On this second sheet, students should add new ideas to the responses of the previous writer.

- Continue this exchange for an agreed-on time limit, giving students opportunities to answer several questions.

- At the conclusion of the activity, have learners retrieve their original papers, review the proposed ideas, and, when appropriate, select one or more solutions to implement or ideas to pursue.

Examples

- After studying the effects of various forms of pollution and proposed solutions, students were asked to pose environmental problems to one another, such as "How can urban storm water runoff pollution be reduced?" and "How can air pollutants from car exhaust be reduced or eliminated?" Based on research done during the environmental unit, solutions generated to the first question included the following:
  o Don't pour oil or grease into a trash bin, storm drain, street, or sanitary sewer.
  o Don't use toxic chemicals such as bleach and detergents to clean trash containers outside.

  A student with less-developed writing skills was able to represent his solutions through pictures and short phrases.

- This activity provides a safe forum for students to discuss sensitive issues. A homeroom teacher, therefore, asked students to react to prompts related to their school and personal lives, such as "Describe a situation in which you felt peer pressure." Students then responded with encouragement or suggestions for their classmates. The teacher also occasionally kept the activity open and gave no prompt, encouraging students to identify anything that might be troubling to them.

Methods to Maximize Engagement and Participation

- Students often need practice writing their problem statement with enough specificity to allow a reader to understand the situation. Consequently, an additional step can be added to allow each person to briefly describe his or her problem before placing it in the center of the table.

- For students with handwriting difficulty, attempting to keep up with the problem exchange could be challenging. The use of assistive technology or augmentative communication supports may be needed for some students to keep pace with classmates. Laptops or tablets can be used by one, some, or all students in these instances. Creating anonymous Google docs to which students add their contributions makes the process paperless and can expedite response time.

IDEAS FOR USING THIS STRUCTURE ✏

_____

_____

_____

_____

_____

_____

_____

_____

_____

_____

_____

_____

_____

_____

AFTER USING THIS STRUCTURE

Did students learn what I intended? Were all students engaged? What changes might be needed to maximize engagement and participation for specific students? How can other team members be involved in co-teaching or instructional support?

_____

_____

_____

_____

_____

_____

_____

_____

_____

_____

_____

_____

_____

_____

_____

Professor Paragraph

Your students don't have to have PhDs to engage in this peer teaching activity, but they do have to be willing to share what they know with others. *Professor Paragraph* allows all learners in the classroom to become experts for the day. It is often useful to use as a review for an upcoming quiz or test. This strategy can boost comprehension of a book, chapter, article, or document, as it can inspire students to read more carefully, identify pieces of the text they understand and those they do not, and engage in repeated readings of the material.

Directions

- Instruct students to briefly review a small section of their textbook or of any other reading selection (e.g., blog post, newspaper article).

- Ask them to find a paragraph (or paragraphs) they understand and could explain to somebody else. Conversely, you can assign each student a different section of the text.

- Instruct students to summarize this material on a large index card.

- When all students have prepared their index cards, ask them to stand and find a partner. Give them two to three minutes to teach their paragraphs to their partners and to have their partners teach their paragraphs to them. After a few minutes, announce, "New partners," and have students repeat the process.

- You can have students change partners once, twice, or several times.

Example

- A social studies teacher used *Professor Paragraph* to teach the US Constitution. Because the document is very long and quite dry, he felt the structure would give students a chance to have a little fun with the content while also providing them opportunities to interpret the text and translate it into contemporary language. Although many of the students chose the same pieces of text to teach (e.g., the Preamble), the teacher viewed the student-to-student interactions as a great opportunity for learners to get multiple interpretations of the document and to, therefore, begin to understand why it is forever being theorized, argued about, and discussed by professors, scholars, lawyers, judges, and even US presidents.

  Two students with learning disabilities were in this classroom. One worked with a teacher to prepare his card. The teacher, acting as a scribe, wrote down the student's responses as the young man shared them verbally. The other student chose to paraphrase his paragraph verbally as homework the night before using a digital audio recorder. This allowed him to listen to his response and practice his summary before sharing it verbally with partners.

Methods to Maximize Engagement and Participation

- Some learners with language and communication difficulties may need to create their cards in advance. Still other learners may need peers to help them construct their cards.

- If many students have difficulties with writing and paraphrasing, you can photocopy the text and allow them to select and cut out the paragraph they will be sharing. To engage in the paraphrasing step of the activity, allow these learners to highlight key words or passages and underline the most important parts of the selection. Students who prefer to engage in this process electronically may want to try apps such as AnnotDoc by EncGoo and Notability by Ginger Labs. These applications or others like them allow users to annotate, highlight, and draw on PDFs.

- For an extra challenge and to boost understanding for some, you can suggest or even require that students illustrate their paragraph. This extra assignment can be beneficial in different ways: It will create interest for artistic and visual students and enhance comprehension for many others, as asking students to draw a complex concept requires them to not only understand the concept they are representing but also consider how to help others understand the concept. Students might even be taught specific visual mapping symbols to use (Margulies & Maal, 2001). These symbols could be taught to and practiced by all students for the purpose of sharing information quickly and efficiently (see Figure 2.7 for examples of symbols that might be adopted in a science class).

Figure 2.7 Possible Visual Mapping Symbols

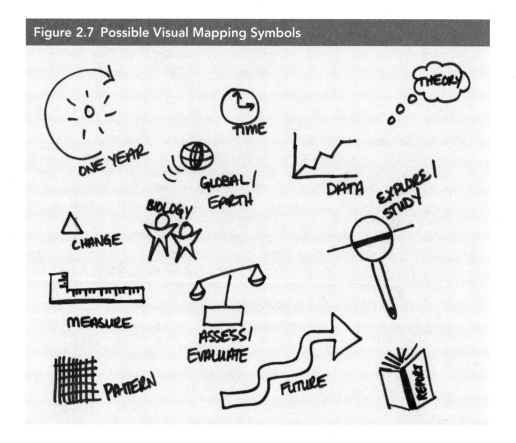

IDEAS FOR USING THIS STRUCTURE

AFTER USING THIS STRUCTURE

Did students learn what I intended? Were all students engaged? What changes might be needed to maximize engagement and participation for specific students? How can other team members be involved in co-teaching or instructional support?

Studying and Reviewing 3

 Draw and Tell

Too often, students assigned a short book, chapter, or long passage get to the end of it and struggle to remember or understand what they have just read. These learners may need opportunities to digest that text in smaller pieces. *Draw and Tell* is an activity that allows readers to do just that; it helps them chunk text into small pieces and promotes retention by engaging students in both drawing and retelling content. It will also, of course, delight your doodlers, sketchers, and cartoonists!

This technique works well with both fictional and informational texts. With fictional texts, this process reinforces structure and the language and imagery of the story; with informational texts, this technique will help students determine what words and details are most important.

Directions

- Give each student one sheet of paper. Instruct them to divide the paper into four even sections by folding it once horizontally and once vertically. Then, have them number each section with a *1* in the upper left hand section, a *2* in the upper right hand section, and so on.

- Begin reading a page, paragraph, or section of text.

- At a designated stopping point (e.g., after three pages), have students stop and think about what you just read. Then, ask them to draw an image related to what they just heard in the first box on the page.

- Start reading once again until you reach a second natural stopping point in the book, chapter, or article.

- Once again, let students draw what they just heard. This time, they will draw in the second box on their page.

- Continue this process until the entire reading has been shared and students have drawn images in all four of the boxes on their page.

- Then, pair students up and instruct them to engage in a retelling using their four pictures. Each student should retell the story or recap the passage using his or her own story map. Give students about five minutes to complete both retellings.

Examples

- In a high school social studies class, students routinely used *Draw and Tell* after listening to their teacher read short articles from *The New York Times*. This process was especially useful when the content was unfamiliar or the vocabulary was potentially challenging for most or all students.

- A student on the autism spectrum could not draw pictures or use a pencil easily, so she worked with a classmate to create a story map for *The Divide*, a book about the life of Willa Cather (see Figure 3.1). As they read, sketched, and created their story maps, the student without identified needs created the pencil drawings, and her classmate colored in some of the images and affixed stickers to add details.

Figure 3.1 *Draw and Tell* Example

Another Version of This Activity

Students can also use *Draw and Learn* when they read on their own. They can read individually, decide on four places in the text they will stop to draw, and engage in the retelling with a partner when both students have finished creating their maps.

Methods to Maximize Engagement and Participation

- Students can be taught to map out the events in an artistic and symbolic way by literally drawing a path or trail and inserting images as they move through the story. Or they can map the content by taking visual notes in chronological order in a notebook or in consecutive boxes on a page.

- Give additional materials to students with motor planning problems. Students who will struggle to draw or to add words and phrases can be given related story stickers or stamps to use in their drawings. Key words and phrases can also be created on a label maker and given to students to "peel and stick" on their papers. Alternatively, you can let these students draw using an app like Microsoft's Paint or Doodle Buddy by Dinopilot.

- Let students create larger or smaller story maps. A short story might require only three opportunities to draw, but it might make sense for learners to create six illustrations for a textbook chapter with exactly six sections.

IDEAS FOR USING THIS STRUCTURE ✎

AFTER USING THIS STRUCTURE

Did students learn what I intended? Were all students engaged? What changes might be needed to maximize engagement and participation for specific students? How can other team members be involved in co-teaching or instructional support?

Save the Last Word for Me

Save the Last Word for Me (Buehl, 1995) is a small-group discussion strategy designed to help students reflect on what they have read and make sense of diverse opinions, interpretations, and viewpoints. Although it was originally designed as a literacy strategy, this technique works well across the curriculum.

Too often in small-group discussions, there is implicit competition for students to be the first to share their information or ideas. As a result, a few speakers may dominate some discussions while others remain more passive or silent. This activity combats these common pitfalls by requiring all participants to submit structured responses before the speaker shares his or her thoughts—thereby, this individual is *saving the last word* for himself or herself.

In *Save the Last Word for Me,* the understandings shared among group members are intended to clarify and deepen any one individual's initial interpretation of the content being discussed. The process can be used across a range of grade levels to prompt conversations in book groups for chapter analysis, to prepare for a debate after reading opinion pieces, or to encourage careful note-taking during research activities. This structure can also be used to debrief films and analyze other visual media such as advertisements, political cartoons, or illustrations. It is an effective complement to the process of close reading (Boyles, 2012/2013), as it can help learners dive deep to discover nuances, details, or connections that may enhance comprehension.

Directions

- Provide the same story, short text, or passage to all students.

- While reading individually, have students find and mark five statements that interest them or to which they would like to react. Selected statements might be something they agree with, disagree with, have heard before, find interesting, or simply want to comment on.

- Distribute index cards to the group. Ask students to write each one of their statements on the front of a card, then flip the card over and write comments they would like to share with the group about the statement on the back of the card.

- Have them repeat this process with each card and each statement.

- Then, put students in small groups and direct them to have one person begin the activity by reading one statement to the group—that is, he or she reads the front of the card but does not provide any thoughts, reflections, or comments on the statement shared. He or she does, however, invite other group members to react to the statement and make comments. Then, when everyone is done commenting, the student who wrote the statement gets "the last word." At this point, he or she can read the back of the card and share additional comments or thoughts on the initial statement.

- A second group member is selected, and the process is repeated.

- Have students engage in this process until all of their cards have been shared and discussed.

Examples

- This strategy was used in a high school social studies class examining historical incidents of hate crimes in America. Groups were given poems from the book *A Wreath for Emmett Till*. Students were asked to select stanzas about the events of the murder that resonated with them, confused them, provided new insight into the historical event, or connected to current issues of racism. As group members responded to each other's selected stanzas, they were able to compare interpretations and learn from the experiences, reflections, and understandings of their peers.

- A ninth-grade algebra teacher used this approach with his daily homework review groups. Students were asked to write one problem that was particularly challenging on one side of the card and their method of problem-solving on the back of the card. Each student had to state how to solve the problem presented, so by the end of each round, students had learned multiple methods for reaching a solution.

Methods to Maximize Engagement and Participation

- Make sure reading selections and, therefore, the related tasks are accessible for all. For example, if a middle school class is reading the novel *Hatchet* by Gary Paulsen, an adapted version of this book—complete with photographs and very simplified text—can be retrieved online at Tar Heel Reader (tarheelreader. org). A student using this version could choose to share either photographs or text excerpts with his or her group.

- Move beyond the book. Use *Save the Last Word for Me* to have students explore graphic novels or poems, websites, songs, or video clips.

- Reduce the rounds of statements from five rounds to only one round.

- Allow students to work with partners. One student might find the items to share while the other articulates interpretations or adds the comments. Students who are emerging readers may need prompts from their partner to participate in the activity. Peers can provide prompts such as these:
  o   Do you want to talk about _____ or _____?
  o   Which illustration do you want to share?

- Adapt the materials. Some students may benefit from having the text highlighted with potential selections from which to choose. Or they may need a set of note cards with relevant points or illustrations from the reading selection already added. These options may make the content more accessible and easier to comprehend.

- Pick a leader. To ensure that group members share their ideas as well as respond to each other, assign the role of facilitator to one member. A sample participation log is shown in Figure 3.2 and can be used by this individual to monitor student contributions.

Figure 3.2 Group Participation Log

Group Participation Log

Use one participation log for each round of *Save the Last Word for Me*. Write each group member's name in a cell in the first column and again in the corresponding cell number of the first row (i.e., if Julie is the first person to begin the round, place her name in cell 1 of the column and cell 1 of the row).

Names	1.	2.	3.	4.	5.
1.	**Shared both sides of note card** **Yes** ___ **No** ___	Gave personal reaction Yes ___ No ___	Gave personal reaction Yes ___ No ___	Gave personal reaction Yes ___ No ___	Gave personal reaction Yes ___ No ___
2.	Gave personal reaction Yes ___ No ___	**Shared both sides of note card** **Yes** ___ **No** ___	Gave personal reaction Yes ___ No ___	Gave personal reaction Yes ___ No ___	Gave personal reaction Yes ___ No ___
3.	Gave personal reaction Yes ___ No ___	Gave personal reaction Yes ___ No ___	**Shared both sides of note card** **Yes** ___ **No** ___	Gave personal reaction Yes ___ No ___	Gave personal reaction Yes ___ No ___
4.	Gave personal reaction Yes ___ No ___	Gave personal reaction Yes ___ No ___	Gave personal reaction Yes ___ No ___	**Shared both sides of note card** **Yes** ___ **No** ___	Gave personal reaction Yes ___ No ___
5.	Gave personal reaction Yes ___ No ___	Gave personal reaction Yes ___ No ___	Gave personal reaction Yes ___ No ___	Gave personal reaction Yes ___ No ___	**Shared both sides of note card** **Yes** ___ **No** ___

Moving to the Music

Get your playlist ready and prepare to see some shaking, shimmying, twisting, and turning. *Moving to the Music* is not only a mood elevator, but it will literally keep your students on their toes. This activity is great for Monday mornings and Friday afternoons alike. In other words, it can be used to wake up a tired classroom or engage excited and energetic students (who might be thinking more about the 3:00 bell than course content) in learning. All you need to engage in *Moving to the Music* is some popular music and a few questions that can be used for discussion or brainstorming.

Directions

- Turn on the music and ask students to begin milling around the room. Tell them they must keep moving and that at this point in the activity talking is not permitted.

- After a few moments, turn the music off.

- Next, direct students to turn to the person who is standing the closest to them. This person will be their partner.

- Use your whiteboard to display a question. Have students turn to their partners and discuss it.

- After a few minutes pass, play the music once again. This is a cue to the group that they should be moving. Let students "move to the music" for a minute or two.

- Then, turn the music off again. Once more, students should turn to the person who is standing closest to them and discuss a question you have assigned.

- Repeat this process until students have had a chance to work with several partners.

- Finally, bring students back to their seats and ask them to discuss ideas they either shared or heard from their partners.

Implementation Tip

You may want to give students some guidelines on how to manage the time given. For instance, if you are going to give them five minutes to discuss each question, ask them to be aware of how much or how little they are speaking. Remind them that they should be speaking for no more or no less than about two-and-a-half minutes in each interaction.

Examples

- A third-grade teacher used this activity at the beginning of the year to learn about the math skills and abilities of his new students. His prompts were as follows:
  - One strategy I use for addition is . . .
  - One strategy I use for subtraction is . . .

    o   When I don't know the answer to a problem, I . . .

    o   When it comes to math, I could use help with . . .

He had students take notes during their meetings so they could potentially learn and remember some new strategies from their peers.

- A creative writing teacher often used *Moving to the Music* to get her students to generate new ideas and to give them new and different ways to get feedback from other writers on ideas they might be developing. One day, to push students into starting a new story, she gave them the topic of *a bank robber* and used the following prompts:

    o   Describe her.

    o   Share at least three details about her past.

    o   Describe the bank she will rob.

    o   What is one plot twist you can envision in this story?

Following the exercise, the teacher had the students go back to their desks immediately and start writing. She asked them to write without "thinking, stopping, editing, or evaluating" for at least 20 minutes.

Occasionally, this teacher involved herself directly in the activity. In these instances, she chose a student to deejay and share the questions. Then, she chose a few students who might need support or guidance and stayed close to them during the game. When the music stopped, she would become the discussion partner for those learners. This strategy allowed her to give and get information and engage in mini-assessments. She used it, in particular, to challenge students but also to check in with two students with learning disabilities who found it difficult to ask and answer content-based questions without a lot of support or preparation.

Methods to Maximize Engagement and Participation

- Take requests! Choose music that students will enjoy or that they might find interesting, or if certain students seem disengaged or disinterested in the activity, you might ask them to choose the music that will be used or even serve as the deejay during the game.

- Bring collaborative partners into the classroom for this one. Therapists, social workers, school psychologists, speech pathologists, and reading specialists may want to "move to the music" with students. Any of these educators can use the structure to have quick meetings with students, engage in skill practice, or assess competencies.

- Have students work on social and communication skills during this game. Have them work on greeting each other, sharing compliments (e.g., "I really like your answer"), staying on topic, or turn taking.

- To draw in your kinesthetic learners, ask students to dance or move in a certain way during the transitions. A teacher who happened to be teaching about Egypt, for instance, asked all students to "walk like Egyptians" as they toured the room. She added to the fun by playing *shaabi*, popular contemporary music of the country.

IDEAS FOR USING THIS STRUCTURE 🖊

_____
_____
_____
_____
_____
_____
_____
_____
_____
_____
_____
_____
_____
_____

AFTER USING THIS STRUCTURE

Did students learn what I intended? Were all students engaged? What changes might be needed to maximize engagement and participation for specific students? How can other team members be involved in co-teaching or instructional support?

_____
_____
_____
_____
_____
_____
_____
_____
_____
_____
_____
_____
_____

Popcorn

Popcorn is controlled chaos at its best. We have so named it because during transitions, students "pop" out of their seats and fly around the room in random directions. *Popcorn* is useful for the times when you want students to share information, teach and learn from each other, and get ideas or opinions from more than one person. It is the perfect choice for lessons that lend themselves to lots of sharing, questioning, and chatting.

Directions

- Begin by instructing students to get "knee to knee, face to face" with one person (this can be done sitting on the floor, standing, or using two chairs).

- Then, have them decide on roles for the activity; one person must be stationary and stay in the same seat or spot for the entire activity. This person is the "kernel," representing the seed that sits in the bottom of the popcorn bowl and does not pop. The other person is mobile and is called "popcorn," as he or she will "pop" up and "fly" around the room during transitions.

- Once roles and names are established, give a prompt or ask a question (e.g., "What do you know about Nicolas II?" and "What are some tools that are used to measure?") and tell the kernels to answer first and to keep talking until you say, "Switch." During this time, popcorn partners are not allowed to speak at all.

- After a minute or so, say, "Switch." At this point, all of those in the popcorn role begin talking; they answer the same question or prompt that the kernels answered. At this time, the kernels should not be speaking and should only be listening.

- After a minute or so, say, "Popcorn." When students hear this, they should abruptly stop speaking. At this point, all of the kernels should stay seated, and all of those in the popcorn role should get up and find an empty chair (or empty spot if you are not using chairs) across from a new kernel.

- Repeat the process.

- Reinforce the rule that students who are listening should *not* speak. They should be silent while their partners share. This rule reminds students that they need to wait for their turn to speak, and it also helps them learn an important aspect of listening—refraining from talking.

Implementation Tip

Ask students to spread out for this activity. Have pairs scattered as far apart from one another as possible to make it easy to see which kernels are "taken" and which ones need partners.

Examples

- An American history teacher used this structure to give learners opportunities to learn from one another and to see the divergence of opinion even in a small class. She asked students who were studying suffrage the following questions:

  o Does voting matter in a democracy? Why or why not?
  o Why do you think some men did not want women to vote?
  o Why do you think some women did not want the right to vote?
  o What risks did the suffragists take?
  o Who are the heroes and heroines of the suffrage movement?

  One student in the classroom had language-based learning disabilities and struggled to generate on-the-spot responses to content-based questions. He was, therefore, put in the popcorn role so he would have a chance to hear his partner answer the questions before he had to answer them.

- A sixth-grade teacher used *Popcorn* to review elements of teamwork with her students. She asked students to answer the following questions in their pairings:

  o What does it mean to be a team player?
  o What does collaboration mean to you?
  o What does negotiation mean to you?
  o How can you be encouraging to your teammates (be specific)?
  o What talents do you bring to a team?

  After the pairs shared their thoughts on each one of the questions, the teacher brought the students back together to engage in a whole-class discussion. She asked them to share some of the things they heard from their classmates. They then drafted a set of guidelines for working in teams that they would use for the entire school year.

  J.P., a student on the autism spectrum who became anxious during this activity, created his own adaptation by asking to be a kernel and to meet with his partner in the hallway. Another student who had low hearing made the same request. Therefore, when students made their switches, they knew they had to scan not only the classroom but also the space outside the room as they looked for new partners.

Methods to Maximize Engagement and Participation

- Assign students who need more "think time" the popcorn role; this way, they will always get to hear their partner share an idea before they are required to do the same.

- Give the prompt and provide a minute of "think time" so that both partners have time to formulate thoughts.

- Some students may feel uncomfortable with this much movement and activity. You might want to allow some of your students to switch partners less frequently or not at all.

- Be sure to allow your most active learners to be in the popcorn role; this will give them teacher-sanctioned opportunities to move.

- Add new roles. If necessary, allow some students to walk around the classroom and listen to conversations before joining in the activity. This role—the "eavesdropper"—can be added to the structure for one round or for the entire activity. Or you can have several students serve as eavesdroppers for the purpose of collecting data on student learning or to observe and encourage the collaborative behaviors of classmates. Another role you might add is that of the "commentator"; this individual adds to conversations or comments on the quality of the conversations (e.g., "You are both doing great with the listening role"). One teacher we observed called students in this role "butter" or "salt," as the commentator often positively "enhances" *Popcorn* conversations!

Another Version of This Activity

Instead of using questions and answers, have students share a piece of writing that is in progress, findings from a final report or project, a solution to a math problem, or concepts they have learned during a unit. In each round of *Popcorn*, students share the same piece of work or teach the same information to a new partner. The opportunity to share or teach the information multiple times provides repeated practice that helps students hone their speaking skills and become more efficient and effective at teaching their content with each subsequent interchange.

For example, at the end of a middle school geology unit, students developed final projects of their choice to convey their understanding of the rock cycle. They wrote poems, raps, and children's books and created informative PowerPoint presentations, cartoon storyboards, and short digital movies. As a culminating activity, students shared their final projects with one another using *Popcorn*. This format was used instead of whole-class presentations, which would have taken additional class sessions. Engaging in *Popcorn* gave each student the undivided attention of several partners and multiple opportunities to improve presentation skills.

IDEAS FOR USING THIS STRUCTURE ✎

_____
_____
_____
_____
_____
_____
_____
_____
_____
_____
_____
_____
_____
_____
_____
_____
_____
_____

AFTER USING THIS STRUCTURE

Did students learn what I intended? Were all students engaged? What changes might be needed to maximize engagement and participation for specific students? How can other team members be involved in co-teaching or instructional support?

_____
_____
_____
_____
_____
_____
_____
_____
_____
_____
_____
_____
_____
_____
_____

Toss-a-Question

Want a novel way to encourage collaboration, support, and the exchange of ideas? Try *Toss-a-Question* (Kagan, 1992). In this structure, students get to ask and answer questions, teach and learn, and share expertise with classmates. Plus, they get to make paper airplanes without being reprimanded! This structure not only works as a tool for reinforcing content, but it is also a quick way to introduce a little levity in learning.

Directions

- Give each student a sheet of paper (or see Figure 3.3 for a worksheet that can be used) and remind them to put their names at the top.

- Tell students to label the top half of the paper *question* and the bottom half of the paper *answer.*

- Then, give them a few minutes to generate a question related to some recently covered content.

- Tell the students that you will know they have finished writing their question when you see that they have crushed their paper into a ball or folded it into an airplane.

- When all students are finished writing, tell them to "toss a question." They should toss their paper across the room. Remind them to be careful to avoid hitting students directly and to aim away from the garbage can. If time permits, have students pick up the papers and toss them again.

- Then, when the commotion clears, invite students to pick up a question, unfold it, and begin generating a response.

- Give students a few minutes to work on their answers. Ask them to crush or fold their papers again.

- Have them toss their papers into the air and retrieve another from the floor one more time. This time, their task is to check the work of the first recipient and add any other information that might help the questioner. If the question is fact based, allow students to use textbooks, websites, notes, or other materials to ensure that they are sharing accurate information.

- Finally, have students toss the questions back to their authors.

- Individual students can then be called on to share their questions and answers.

Implementation Tip

If you don't want the commotion and chaos of papers flying through the air, this activity can be carried out in a more controlled (albeit less exciting) fashion by having students toss all of their questions onto a table and retrieve a paper from the bunch. You can also make the exchange less messy by having students make eye contact with a single partner and gently exchange papers via a short person-to-person toss.

Figure 3.3 *Toss-a-Question*: Q & A Worksheet

Toss-a-Question

Name of Question Writer _____

Name of Answer Writer _____

Name of Answer Checker _____

Question:

Answer:

Examples

- Students in an eleventh-grade English class were asked to toss discussion questions related to the novel they were studying—*Night* by Elie Wiesel. Questions included these:
  - o How did Wiesel survive such adversity?
  - o What does the title of this book mean?
  - o Wiesel writes often of fathers and sons. Why is this an important theme in the book?

  Students tossed their questions to partners, and the teacher gave the recipients more than 10 minutes to develop responses. Students then tossed the questions a second time, and that recipient filled in missing information, added details, or offered another opinion.

- In a fourth-grade classroom in Massachusetts, students were studying their home state. The teacher had students ask and answer questions about their favorite things in the state. The questions were to be open-ended and were not to be based on facts but on student preferences. As an example, she shared the question "What is your favorite tourist attraction in Massachusetts?" and tossed it to a student who volunteered that she loved going to the Freedom Trail, an attraction that features historical sites relevant to the American Revolution. That student then tossed the question to another student, who also had to answer the question. Students had their questions tossed around the room five times and then returned to them as a piece of data they could use in upcoming reports on the region.

Another Version of This Activity

Instead of using questions and answers, have students work on a collaborative piece using this structure. For instance, a middle school language arts teacher had students write a collective poem by asking one learner to write a line and then toss it to another, who would add a line and toss it again. Stories, fact sheets, brainstorming lists, essays, sheet music, drawings, and many other products can be constructed in this way.

Methods to Maximize Engagement and Participation

- If particular students will struggle to write their own question on the paper, they might be provided a set of prewritten questions on sticky notes. Their task is to read the questions and choose one for the exercise. The sticky note can then be attached to the paper. If writing is not a problem, you could also provide the students a list of potential questions and allow them to copy their question onto the sheet.

- Play music as students toss papers. If students are tossing paper airplanes, you might use "Come Fly With Me" by Frank Sinatra. If they are tossing snowballs, try "Let It Snow."

- Once the papers are tossed, let students work with a partner to answer their respective questions; this may help to ensure accuracy and inspire more thoughtful answers.

- To challenge particular students, get in on the game. Create enrichment questions that are especially difficult and identify certain students who will receive their "toss" from the teacher.

- Use this activity to teach students to write questions at different levels of complexity. Some examples follow:

  o At the recall level: What number is the denominator in this fraction?
  o At the application level: What are two fractions between 2/3 and 3/4?
  o At the analysis level: Which of these drawings illustrate a fraction as a part of a set, and which illustrate a fraction as a part of a whole?

Bloom's Revised Taxonomy can be a helpful tool to craft questions at different levels of understanding. A resource with question stems at each level of the taxonomy can be found at http://facultycenter.ischool.syr.edu/wp-content/uploads/2015/10/Revised-Blooms-Questions-Starter.pdf.

IDEAS FOR USING THIS STRUCTURE

AFTER USING THIS STRUCTURE

Did students learn what I intended? Were all students engaged? What changes might be needed to maximize engagement and participation for specific students? How can other team members be involved in co-teaching or instructional support?

Guess Who?

Don't just study Sitting Bull, let students *be* Sitting Bull. For that matter, let them be Charles Lindbergh, Sylvia Plath, Cesar Chavez, Anne Sullivan, Sally Ride, Georgia O'Keeffe, or Thomas Edison. *Guess Who?* gives students an opportunity to be someone or something notable or interesting, and it allows them to meet others who are notable and interesting. Not studying any of these figures in your classroom? Don't worry! This activity is flexible and will also let students "become" things such as rain forests, erosion, and prime numbers.

Although this game takes some up-front planning, once the materials are constructed and the rules are learned the exercise can be repeated several times. The best part? Students can take on new identities every time they play.

Directions

- Using mailing or address labels, create a set of adhesive tags with names, concepts, ideas, or definitions written on them—for example, a geometry teacher might create a set with a different shape on each (e.g., rhombus, cuboid).

- Attach a label to each student's back (or forehead if you want to be a bit silly) showing everyone—except the person wearing the label—what is written on it.

- The player with the label on his or her back (who does not know what is written on the label) must then ask closed-ended questions (requiring only yes or no answers) to establish his or her identity. Using the aforementioned geometry example, a student might ask questions such as "Am I a triangle?" or "Do I have straight lines?"

- This structure, although often used for amusement alone, can help students think in complex ways about course content. Figuring out one's identity in this game requires critical thinking and attention to detail. If you are trying to figure out your shape, for instance, you need to determine what elements in particular separate different types of shapes (e.g., tools used to draw them, lines or lack thereof, types of angles involved if any). Engaging in this type of categorization gets students thinking a bit "outside the box" and can enhance students' comprehension of a particular concept.

Examples

- One high school chemistry teacher used this game during a lesson on the periodic table. Each student had one element stuck to his or her back and had to ask questions such as these:
  - Am I a solid?
  - Am I a liquid?
  - Am I heavy?
  - Am I inert?
  - Are the letters of my symbol part of my name?

One student in the classroom who needed extra challenge during this unit was given the role of "Guess Guru"; he was responsible for helping struggling students come up with good questions to narrow the field of possibilities. When one student was stumped and could not guess his element, the Guess Guru came up with the questions "Am I used for nuclear fission?" and "Does my element begin with a *P?*" When the student got "yes" answers to the questions, he was able to correctly guess that the element was plutonium.

- A tenth-grade English teacher used *Who Is It?* to help students learn and remember the characters in *The Great Gatsby*. To provide each student with a unique label and to make the activity more challenging, she included story characters (e.g., Gatsby, Daisy), story symbols (e.g., flowers, ashes), and story ideas (e.g., nouveau riche) in the game. The teacher made a slight adaptation in the activity for a young woman with intellectual disabilities in the classroom. The students played the game twice (once when they were halfway through the novel and once when they were finished), and both times, this student was assigned a character (not a symbol or an idea). The student worked with a peer to review character traits and descriptions on a few different occasions and rehearsed a few questions in advance with a paraprofessional in the classroom. She was, therefore, able to guess her character both times by using simple questions such as "Am I a male or female?" and "Do I die?" and "Am I rich?"

Methods to Maximize Engagement and Participation

- Pair pictures with words on the labels for students who may be emerging readers.

- Some students may need a "starter" set of questions for the activity; give those learners a few options to use as they begin the exercise (e.g., "Am I a person, place, or thing?").

- Ask students to generate the set of labels that will be used in the activity. You can assign this as an enrichment activity for students needing more challenge, or you can ask all students to work with a partner and generate two labels to add to the classroom set.

- Give a "sponge" activity to students who guess their identity early in the activity. Instruct them to sit down immediately and to write down at least three things they learned from the questions and answers provided.

- Consider adding additional roles to the activity; some students can walk around the room giving hints to the askers and answerers, and others can simply observe and record information that is passed from person to person.

IDEAS FOR USING THIS STRUCTURE ✎

AFTER USING THIS STRUCTURE

Did students learn what I intended? Were all students engaged? What changes might be needed to maximize engagement and participation for specific students? How can other team members be involved in co-teaching or instructional support?

 Hot Seat

Get your students fired up with a round or two of this unique cooperative teaching technique! *Hot Seat* provides a fast-paced way to engage a whole class in skill or information drills. It also can be used to gather information from each member of the class in an efficient manner that promotes face-to-face interaction. In addition, because this structure requires students to work with several different partners, *Hot Seat* is a great "get-to-know-you" activity for the first day of class.

Directions

- Position students in two rows (with these rows facing one another). Inform students that one row will act as the "interrogators" (or "questioners" if you prefer a more friendly term), and the other row will act as the "informants" and sit in the "hot seats" (because they will be questioned by each of the interrogators).

- Give each interrogator a question. Or give the interrogators time to generate a question of their own. Each interrogator must have a different question.

- Begin the game by asking the interrogators to share their questions with their partners. After the questions are posed, the informants should answer the questions as completely as possible.

- After the pairs have had a few minutes to ask and answer their questions, announce, "Next question." At this point, informants stand up and move down one chair in the row. The informant at the end of the row stands up and moves to the chair at the front or top of the row. Once all informants are sitting down again, the interrogators repeat their questions.

- After every informant has answered every question, have students switch roles—that is, the interrogators should change positions and become informants. Questions can remain the same or be changed for the second round.

Implementation Tip

This structure can be particularly beneficial for students who need multiple trials to learn or memorize information. Place these students in the interrogator seats first, so they are able to hear answers to the questions repeated several times.

Examples

- A high school biology teacher used this technique to review content that had been missed on an exam. Each student reviewed his or her exam individually and created a question-and-answer card for an incorrect item. The cards were distributed to the interrogators. Therefore, at some point in the rotation, each person heard and responded to the question card that he or she developed.

- Several elementary school teachers used this technique to teach data collection and graphing. Each interrogator developed a question that allowed multiple responses (e.g., "What is your favorite color?"). During the activity, each interrogator was given a graph to chart the responses of each person who sat in the hot seat. At the end of the activity, data had been gathered and graphed on at least 20 different questions. The class analyzed the data to determine high- and low-frequency responses by the class.

Another Version of This Activity

Rather than having the students in the hot seat rotate, the questions used by the interrogators can be passed down the row so that each pair receives a new prompt to ask about and answer after each exchange.

Methods to Maximize Engagement and Participation

- The teacher or students can develop the questions used by the interrogators, or you can structure the activity so that learners answer some teacher-created questions and a few of their own. After a few rounds of teacher-generated questions, tell students they need to generate a related question for each informant.

- Students who may need more practice with the information can remain in the position of interrogators instead of switching roles midway through the game.

- Use a cue to signal students to move. This may speed up the process and add some whimsy to the game. Instead of saying, "Next question," you could play a game show song clip, shut the lights on and off, or ring a bell.

- If some students will be uncomfortable working in such a large group, smaller rows of interrogators and informants can be formed. For example, in a classroom of 24 students, instead of having one row of 12 and another row of 12, you could have two *Hot Seat* rotations going on at the same time, with two rows of six working on one side of the room and two rows of six working on the other side of the room.

IDEAS FOR USING THIS STRUCTURE ✏

AFTER USING THIS STRUCTURE

Did students learn what I intended? Were all students engaged? What changes might be needed to maximize engagement and participation for specific students? How can other team members be involved in co-teaching or instructional support?

Say Something

Short, Harste, and Burke (1996) developed this shared reading strategy, which promotes comprehension and construction of meaning from text. In *Say Something*, students read a piece of text together, and then at various points, they stop and exchange thoughts about what has been read. Learners are encouraged to look for relationships between new information and their existing knowledge.

This active reading structure can be particularly helpful for students who have comprehension difficulties and for those who are unable or unlikely to read material outside of class. *Say Something* ensures that all students are on the "same page," so to speak, and that they have opportunities to both give and get support.

Directions

- Select a piece of text that ranges in length from a few sentences to a few pages.

- Place students in pairs and give each pair of students the reading selection.

- Tell students they will be reading the text as a team. Direct them to glance at the text and decide on a handful of places where they will stop and "say something" to one another. In these spots, they may share a question, make a point, connect the information to personal experience, note something that was particularly interesting, or paraphrase what was read.

- Ask them to begin reading. Remind them to repeat the process of stopping, sharing, and starting until they finish the selection.

- Move around the room during the activity to ensure that students remain on topic. You may also need to monitor the length of the *Say Something* exchanges. Students should make brief comments to one another rather than launching into debates or long discussions.

- After all pairs have completed the selection, facilitate a whole-group discussion about the text.

Implementation Tip

When teaching students to engage in this strategy, it may be necessary to demonstrate the process and develop a list or menu of different ways to "say something."

Examples

- In a unit comparing creationism and evolution, a high school science teacher used this technique with two short readings—one an excerpt from a religious text and the other an essay by Richard Leakey, famed archeologist—to spark interest and controversy on the first day of instruction. Students were encouraged to share brief comments during the shared reading exercise and save longer comments and questions for the whole-class portion of the activity.

- Before a fifth-grade class was to attend a performance of *Peter and the Wolf,* the teacher asked students to listen to short segments of the symphony. Students were asked to pay attention to how the music portrayed the characters, the dynamics of the piece (loudness and softness), and the tempo. They were then cued to turn to a partner in the class and "say something" about the different elements featured in the lesson. To demonstrate how to engage in the activity, the teacher modeled the structure with a student who was a talented musician and was also legally blind. This student's complex answers about the composer's choices (e.g., he noted that all of the characters are represented by a certain instrument) stunned classmates who didn't know about his musical prowess; it also helped them learn more about the play and about the collaborative structure they were using.

- A middle school art teacher used this technique to introduce the surrealist painting styles of Remedios Varo, Marc Chagall, and Salvador Dali. Each student pair was given a series of pictures by the artists. The teacher used a three-minute egg timer to create a "viewing window" for each assigned painting. At each three-minute interval, the teacher cued students to stop and "say something" to their partners. Afterward, the teacher asked them to comment on their emotional responses to the pictures, on the common or dissimilar styles of painting, and on the possible hidden messages intended by the artists.

Another Version of This Activity

Add a little novelty and mystery to the game by introducing a *Say Something* cube that directs students to share a particular type of response. To play, create a cube with a different question or prompt on each of the six sides. You might use prompts such as the following:

- I predict that . . .
- I think that . . .
- Since _____ happened, I wonder if _____ will also happen.
- I bet the next thing that is going to happen is . . .
- Reading this part makes me think that _____ is about to happen.
- I wonder if . . .

Want help? A customizable cube creator is available from ReadWriteThink at www .readwritethink.org/classroom-resources/student-interactives/cube-creator-30850 .html.

Methods to Maximize Engagement and Participation

- As noted in the previous examples, *Say Something* can be used with non-text material. The activity can be structured with one student examining text on a topic and the other examining visual media (e.g., photos, pictures). At an agreed-on time frame (e.g., after examining the materials for three minutes), students can stop and "say something." *Note:* Even the best readers in class should occasionally be given non-text material and different types of reading materials (e.g., comic books, picture books) to reinforce that information can be gained from many sources.

- Students may also be paired with readings on the same topic but at different reading levels. At the stopping points, students share what they have gained from their text.

- One person in the partnership can read the text aloud. This is not a fluency technique, but a comprehension technique, so it is appropriate to allow one student to read the text to his or her partner if this is preferred.

- If two students read at different paces, the student who completes the reading first can write down and elaborate on his or her *Say Something* comment while his or her partner completes the reading.

- Both students can keep a running list of comments and questions that have been generated and use it during the whole-class discussion. This list can also serve as an accountability tool, as it provides evidence of student participation.

- When a student uses a communication board, pictures, or symbols to communicate, he can participate by making comments or posing questions (e.g., "That was interesting" or "I didn't understand that" or "Can you put that in your own words?"). To teach and reinforce the use of the communication system, both students might be encouraged to use the system to comment on the text.

IDEAS FOR USING THIS STRUCTURE ✎

_____
_____
_____
_____
_____
_____
_____
_____
_____
_____
_____
_____
_____
_____
_____
_____

AFTER USING THIS STRUCTURE

Did students learn what I intended? Were all students engaged? What changes might be needed to maximize engagement and participation for specific students? How can other team members be involved in co-teaching or instructional support?

_____
_____
_____
_____
_____
_____
_____
_____
_____
_____
_____
_____
_____
_____
_____

Cracking the Code

When many of us were in school, drawing on our papers was viewed as a sign of inattention. Writing anything on our textbooks was usually followed with a reprimand. Times have changed, and teachers understand that students need to highlight, underline, and make notes on their papers or electronic texts. However, these responses are still not encouraged enough or with an instructional purpose. *Crack the Code* empowers students to mark up their papers and electronic texts with a variety of graphic codes to communicate their understandings, questions, and epiphanies. This strategy can be used to check students' understanding of assigned readings, directions, concepts in the text, or homework problems.

Directions

- Provide students with a chapter, piece of text, or mathematical problem set.

- Ask them to draw codes or insert codes in the margins that convey their understanding of the material. The codes should be designed to reflect different responses to the material. For example, codes can include marks such as these:
  - A check mark (to signify understanding—"I get this")
  - A question mark (to signify misunderstandings—"I'm not sure about this concept", "I don't understand what the author is trying to say", "The vocabulary is difficult", or "This equation is very confusing to me")
  - An exclamation point (to signify points of interest or that the student understands the material well—"I *really* get this!" "I'd like to talk about this point!" "I could teach this to someone else!")

- Allow students to code worksheets, books they own, or copies of material. They can also use note-taking apps and tablets if they have access to devices.

- Give students time to review their own codes and the codes used by a few peers sitting near them. Some students who coded that they understood material well can explain their thinking to others. Teachers and students should be alert to material that was coded as misunderstood or confusing to multiple students. These common points of misunderstanding should be the focus of further instruction.

Implementation Tip

When textbooks are used, the student can code with sticky notes. A set of these notes could be saved and used for multiple applications.

Examples

- After outlining procedures for the day and prior to engaging in a science lab, an instructor asked students to read the directions for the day's activities and examine each of the tasks to be completed. He asked students to use just two codes: a check mark, indicating that "I understand what to do," and a question mark, meaning "I'm kind of confused about this." The instructor then moved around the room, silently viewing the codes. This assessment alerted him that a number of students were confused by vocabulary in one step of the procedure. Consequently, he took a moment to explain that procedure in detail. He also provided assistance to groups with members who registered confusion with their codes.

A benefit to this process was that after listening to verbal directions, the students were focused and attentive as they read the directions. As a result, the teacher noticed there were fewer misunderstandings and random questions during the lab.

- A calculus teacher used this strategy prior to giving a homework assignment. She asked students to preview the assigned problems and code them for understanding. She discovered that several students felt very confident in their abilities to solve a particular problem. Before ending class, she asked these students to demonstrate the problem while the rest of the class took notes. The homework was then reduced by one problem.

Another Version of This Activity

Instead of having students use codes to signify understanding, use them to encourage strategic note-taking. Begin by having students divide their papers into four quadrants or columns. An icon should be drawn in each of the four sections:

- A light bulb (representing new ideas)

- A key (representing "key" ideas)

- A question mark (representing things that are still confusing)

- A face or stick figure (representing concepts they want to discuss with others)

As you give a lecture or facilitate a whole-class discussion, encourage students to record new information in the appropriate boxes. This structure can make it easier for some learners to identify points of interest, areas of difficulty, or confusion with the content.

Students can also be asked to generate additional icons to help them organize their notes and make the content more memorable.

Methods to Maximize Engagement and Participation

- This technique can be used during a lecture. Provide the class with small whiteboards. A few times during the lecture, ask for a "code of understanding" from the group. At this point, have students hold up their whiteboards and display a symbol that indicates their level of comprehension.

- *Crack the Code* can be used as a strategy for cultivating peer support. Teachers can have all students read a piece of text and code it. Based on the codes, the teacher can spontaneously put students in teaching-and-learning pairs to ask and answer questions.

- Introduce other graphic note-taking options to students—for example, you might show students examples of mind mapping, sketchnoting, and graphic facilitation. Teach students techniques and vocabulary "words," and share materials they might use (e.g., bullet journals, colored pencils, 3-D markers) to engage in these methods.

- Give alternatives to paper and pencil. Let students take notes using their tablets and develop codes using color, highlights, and icons. Introduce apps for note-taking and annotation, such as Sketchbook Express by Autodesk Inc. and Notability by Ginger Labs.

IDEAS FOR USING THIS STRUCTURE ✏

AFTER USING THIS STRUCTURE

Did students learn what I intended? Were all students engaged? What changes might be needed to maximize engagement and participation for specific students? How can other team members be involved in co-teaching or instructional support?

Match Game

Match Game requires students to interact in a structured way to teach and learn from their classmates. It is the perfect antidote to dry, dull, drill-and-practice exercises. It can be particularly helpful for teaching and reviewing facts, dates, vocabulary, and definitions.

This structure gets students out of their seats and helps even the most struggling learner succeed. If that student cannot find the right answer, the answer may find him or her!

Directions

- Make two groups of cards (A and B); each card in one group (A) must have a matching card in the other group (B). For instance, you might create one group of questions (A) and one group of answers (B), one group of words (A) and one group of definitions (B), or one group of incomplete sentences (A) and one group of words or phrases that complete the sentences (B).

- Then, give every student one card.

- Tell the students to walk around the room, talk to other students, and compare their cards with the cards of their classmates. Once students have found the card and the individual who matches their own, they should sit down next to that person and wait for others to find their matches.

- When all students have found matches, ask each pair to share their match with the class. Pairs can simply read their cards to the others or quiz the rest of the class using the information they have learned from their match (e.g., "My card is 9 x 9. Can you guess what is on Lacy's card?").

Implementation Tip

To keep students engaged after they have found their matches, put related information, trivia, or "brain buster" questions on the back of cards. This way, students can discuss this additional content while they wait for all other students to pair up.

Examples

- One teacher used *Match Game* to showcase the talents of Marn, one of her students on the autism spectrum who was interested in trains. During a unit on transportation, this student created one set of cards that contained phrases related to trains. On another set of cards, she wrote the corresponding definitions. One card, for instance, had the phrase *run-through* written on it. The definition of *run-through*, which is "a train that generally is not scheduled to pick up or reduce (set out) railcars en route," was written on another card.

  Students had to find matches for terms and phrases that were, in most cases, completely new to them. They had fun learning the new lingo and were impressed with their classmate's expertise in this area. According to the teacher, the game was the first opportunity students had to go to this learner to get help and information. This experience changed students' perceptions of Marn and inspired others in the classroom to "show off" their own special knowledge by designing a set of *Match Game* cards.

- After writing research reports and preparing posters on self-selected topics, fifth graders were encouraged by their teacher to design active learning strategies to keep their audience attentive and engaged when they presented their findings to the class. One student in the class, Madda, used this technique. Madda's report featured cultural customs and artists of Mexico. To prepare for her presentation, she made *Match Game* cards representing various concepts and facts she wanted her audience to learn from her report. One set of cards displayed questions or definitions, and the other set contained answers or terms.

The teacher encouraged Madda to make cards that would ensure everyone's participation and understanding. Since some students in the classroom were emerging readers, Madda constructed several cards that included pictures and photographs as clues. These same images were also represented on her poster. She distributed cards to her classmates at the start of the presentation, so they could be listening for the information required for their success in the game. At the end of the presentation, students had to find their matches. Several students confirmed their matches by comparing their cards to the images and text on her poster. Figure 3.4 shows a sample of the *Match Game* cards created for this project.

Figure 3.4 Sample *Match Game* Cards Used in a Student Presentation

Altar

An offering of food, flowers, and treats for the dead.

This is a picture of Frida and ?

Library of Congress, Prints & Photographs Division, Carl Van Vechten Collection, [reproduction number, e.g., LC-USZ62-54231]

Diego Rivera

Methods to Maximize Engagement and Participation

- Have some students participate in creating the cards. As in our aforementioned examples, being the creator of an activity will be especially rewarding for a student who has a unique area of expertise, such as trains, rodeos, South America, or spelunking.

- Encourage students to support each other during the game. Remind them that they can give clues to their classmates to help them find matches. You could even demonstrate how learners can give support. Show them, for instance, how to give clues (but not answers) to classmates or how to ask clarifying questions of one another.

- Color code the cards or add stylized text for some students so they can narrow down the number of individuals they need to approach as potential matches. For instance, a teacher using this structure to practice Spanish vocabulary might have all of the words in white and all of the definitions in pink. Furthermore, all of the verbs might be in italics. Therefore, a student assigned a card with the word *salta* printed on it knows that he or she needs to approach only those with pink cards that also have italicized text.

IDEAS FOR USING THIS STRUCTURE

_____
_____
_____
_____
_____
_____
_____
_____
_____
_____
_____
_____
_____
_____
_____
_____
_____

AFTER USING THIS STRUCTURE

Did students learn what I intended? Were all students engaged? What changes might be needed to maximize engagement and participation for specific students? How can other team members be involved in co-teaching or instructional support?

_____
_____
_____
_____
_____
_____
_____
_____
_____
_____
_____
_____
_____
_____

Paper Bag Interviews

In today's busy standards-based classrooms, students have less time than ever before to socialize and to ask and answer questions about life both inside and outside of school. *Paper Bag Interviews* (Gibbs, 1995) can be used regularly throughout the year to give students such opportunities. Students tend to enjoy the I-wonder-what-I'm-going-to-draw suspense and the community-building nature of the activity.

Directions

- Write a series of questions and place them in small, brown, paper lunch bags.

- Put students into small groups; hand each one a bag.

- Direct them to take turns drawing questions from the bag and answering them. At any point, a student may decide to pass on a question and draw a new one.

- Use this activity to give students opportunities to learn personal information about one another or to comment on different topics of study in the classroom. Questions can also prompt students to both share personal stories and reflect on curriculum—for example, "How are you most like Crazy Horse?" prompts students to disclose something about themselves while they consider information they have about this historical figure.

Example

- A middle school earth science teacher regularly used *Paper Bag Interviews* as a content review and as a way to facilitate positive working relationships in the classroom. During a unit on earthquakes, he included the following questions in his "interview bags":
  - What is a tsunami?
  - If someone gave you a beautiful house in an area known for earthquakes, would you make your home there? Why or why not?
  - Name the three types of earthquake waves.
  - How do you think city planning and building construction will change in the next 50 years in earthquake zones?
  - What is one way individuals, a city, or the federal government can minimize the damage of an earthquake?
  - What is the most interesting thing about earthquakes you have learned in this unit?
  - Explain the difference between a focus and an epicenter.

  To differentiate instruction for this activity, the teacher included a few "pink slips" in the bag. Students knew these brightly colored questions would be more challenging and abstract than the others. Any student was invited to choose a pink-slip question, but if he or she could not answer it, others in the group were allowed to try.

Methods to Maximize Engagement and Participation

- Color code the questions so students can make a choice based on their mood, skill level, or preference. Different colors could be used, for instance, for questions that are more personal in nature, more silly, or more serious, or they could be coded for level of difficulty.

- Put questions in the bags that relate to student interests. If a student in the group has just become an uncle, include a question about this big event. If a student is really interested in the Beatles, include a question about rock and roll in the 1960s.

- If you have some students in your class with communication differences, you might add some interest to the activity if you ask all students to take turns answering questions using different types of augmentative communication, such as sign language, gestures, and pictures.

- If students in the classroom receive support from a speech and language therapist, *Paper Bag Interviews* offer a perfect opportunity for coteaching or collaborative consultation. A therapist might work in the classroom during this activity and help all students improve skills such as asking appropriate questions and staying on topic.

- If you really want to be purposeful in what types of questions each student answers, you can put names on individual questions, and as each learner draws a slip of paper, he or she reads the question to the learner who has been assigned it.

IDEAS FOR USING THIS STRUCTURE ✎

_____

_____

_____

_____

_____

_____

_____

_____

_____

_____

_____

_____

_____

_____

_____

_____

AFTER USING THIS STRUCTURE

Did students learn what I intended? Were all students engaged? What changes might be needed to maximize engagement and participation for specific students? How can other team members be involved in co-teaching or instructional support?

_____

_____

_____

_____

_____

_____

_____

_____

_____

_____

_____

_____

_____

_____

Human Continuum

Human Continuum allows teachers to quickly view student perspectives. You can use it to explore questions of ethics, opinions, viewpoints, understandings, and interests. It also gives students opportunities to literally see where they stand on issues as compared with their peers. This structure works as a way to learn about student knowledge but can also serve as a values clarification exercise.

Directions

- Begin by showing students a five-point Likert-type scale.

- After providing some "think time," ask them to choose the number that best describes their position on an issue (e.g., "I understand how to multiply binomials"; "I feel animal cloning is ethical").

- Be sure to indicate the values for the scale—for example, if you want *1* to represent *disagree* and *2* to represent *disagree somewhat,* and so on, then post those labels on the Likert-type scale visual.

- Next, tell students you are going to make a life-size scale. Pick a wall and label one corner "1" and the other "5." Then, ask students to find the place on the wall that matches their response.

- Then, randomly ask students to share their perspectives. You might begin by asking a student on the high end of the continuum, a student on the lower end of the continuum, and a student in the middle of the continuum to report on what their views are and why they chose their spots.

Examples

- In a middle school social studies class, the teacher asked students to respond to the following statements using *Human Continuum;* those who *strongly agreed* with the statement stood near the number *5,* those who *strongly disagreed* with the statement stood by the number *1,* and all others stood somewhere in between, depending on their views:
  - John Adams is an American hero.
  - Colonists were justified in destroying property during the Boston Tea Party to gain political attention.
  - Women played an important role in the American Revolution.
  - Benedict Arnold was a traitor.
  - The American Revolution was a necessary war.

  As students made their choices and shuffled into line in their appropriate spots, the teacher called on individuals to share the rationale for their choices. When he found two or more learners with strong feelings at the opposite ends of the continuum, he asked them to engage in a short, friendly debate in front of the class.

- In a fifth-grade classroom, the teacher used *Human Continuum* as a way to kick off a unit on nutrition. She told the students they would use the exercise as a way to assess their knowledge, behavior, and beliefs and as a way to compare their lifestyle and habits with others their own age. She asked students to respond to the following prompts:

o I eat a balanced diet.
o I think it is important to learn about good nutrition.
o I can prepare a healthy snack.
o I know what appropriate portion sizes look like for someone my size and weight.
o I think exercise is important.
o I like to eat fruits and vegetables.
o I eat too much junk food.
o I think advertising influences my food choices.

Another Version of This Activity

This activity lends itself well to paired discussion. To form dyads in which students can exchange viewpoints on the topics, have them line up based on their position on any issue. Then, break the line at the midpoint and "fold" it so that the two students at each end are paired, and so on (e.g., 1 and 20 pair, 2 and 19 pair, 3 and 18 pair). Pairing students of opposing viewpoints can prepare them to work on skills such as active listening and perspective taking.

Methods to Maximize Engagement and Participation

- Some students may have a hard time forming an opinion immediately; these learners might be given some time in advance to write a response, or you might choose to give all students time to construct a quick response to the prompts, therefore giving everyone some practice in written expression and, specifically, in forming and defending an opinion.

- Write the numbers *1* through *5* in large print on chart paper, and post these numbers along the wall so students see exactly where the markers are for each digit.

- To further help students clarify their positions, you might ask them to add decimals to their responses. Learners can then declare that they are a 1.5 as opposed to a 1.6 on a particular issue (might be an especially helpful addition for teachers of mathematics). To take the math practice a step further, you might even assign one or two students as "number crunchers." Their job is to observe the line and average the score of the class on each point.

IDEAS FOR USING THIS STRUCTURE ✐

_____
_____
_____
_____
_____
_____
_____
_____
_____
_____
_____
_____
_____
_____
_____
_____
_____
_____
_____

AFTER USING THIS STRUCTURE

Did students learn what I intended? Were all students engaged? What changes might be needed to maximize engagement and participation for specific students? How can other team members be involved in co-teaching or instructional support?

_____
_____
_____
_____
_____
_____
_____
_____
_____
_____
_____
_____
_____
_____
_____
_____
_____

Creating Active Lectures 4

Lectures Alive

Students so often groan when they know they are in store for a long classroom lecture. They may have a very different reaction, however, if they are involved in teaching the lesson and collaborating to make learning more enjoyable and engaging.

This one takes a little time to plan, but you will be glad you made the investment once you see your students illustrating, informing, and imparting instead of slumping, sleeping, and shrugging!

Directions

- Give every student in the classroom a card containing a fact, quote, thought, idea, or illustration.

- Ask the group to study their cards and engage in a few minutes of informal research on the facts, thoughts, or ideas they have been assigned.

- Then, begin your lecture on the topic. At different points, stop and invite students to come forward to present the information they have been assigned. Some students might come forward and just recite a fact. Others might give a quick description of an event. Still others might chant an important phrase.

- During the course of a lecture or discussion, try to involve every student and his or her contribution.

Implementation Tip

Once students have assignments, you might want to give them a little time to do their own research on their fact, quote, thought, or idea. This may allow them to make a more informed contribution and to ad lib a bit when they are called upon to share.

Example

- During a lecture on the United States Supreme Court, a high school teacher used *Lectures Alive* to involve every student in the classroom. He introduced the current Supreme Court by asking the nine students with photos and bios of the justices to come forward and highlight them one by one. Other students were brought up at different points in the lecture. One student shared information about the role of the chief justice. Three students had signs that simply read *executive branch,* and every time this term was mentioned, they were asked to stand up and say, "Executive branch." A few students had information to share on landmark cases, so each time one of these was outlined, a different student stood to give a few details on it. During the 45-minute lecture, every student in the classroom served as a collaborator.

Methods to Maximize Engagement and Participation

- Give students with more ability and interest in a particular topic more responsibility during certain lectures. Some students may want to do more than read from a card. These learners may want to explain a concept, present a diagram, provide relevant examples, or lead an activity.

- It is not necessary for every student to make a verbal contribution. Some students may want to hold up photographs or diagrams or take part in a demonstration instead.

- Learners with anxiety or others who would find it intimidating to stand in front of the classroom might be given an opportunity to create a video clip to share with classmates. The clip could then be integrated into the lecture.

- Ask students how they want to participate in lectures. Find out which students like to take "doodle notes" as you talk, which might want to participate in impromptu skits, and which would want to chant and cheer to help their classmates remember a concept, phrase, or important vocabulary word.

IDEAS FOR USING THIS STRUCTURE

AFTER USING THIS STRUCTURE

Did students learn what I intended? Were all students engaged? What changes might be needed to maximize engagement and participation for specific students? How can other team members be involved in co-teaching or instructional support?

Up and Down

If you are looking for an alternative to a "raise-your-hand-if-you-know" format, this activity is for you. *Up and Down* is a playful way to hear from a wide range of students in a short period of time. This structure can be used in two ways; it can serve as a tool for reflection, and it can give students opportunities to listen with purpose. Further, the game suggests to students that both sharing and listening are valued. The "up-and-down" nature of the activity also serves to "shake up" a traditional classroom discussion so that those needing novelty, movement, or interaction can get just a bit of all three of those things.

Directions

- Present a prompt or question to the group and invite students to share brief responses to it.

- Tell the group that you will need one student to hop up and start the activity. This individual should provide a quick response and sit down when he or she finishes speaking.

- Encourage others to add to the initial comment. Students who want to share should decide where their comment best fits into the discussion and stand when they feel they want to make their contribution. When a speaker sits down, this is the signal for the next person who wishes to stand and share.

- If two students stand at the same time, encourage them to decide between them who will speak first.

- Remind all speakers to be brief (e.g., under one minute).

- After several students have stood up to share their thoughts, turn to those who are sitting down and ask this group to comment on what they just heard. They will not make remarks about the original prompt; they will focus on what those who stood up said, shared, and discussed. They can choose to summarize what a few students have said, or they can paraphrase or comment on what just one classmate shared.

- Again, let students direct the activity and decide when to share.

- After several students in the second group have shared, summarize the discussion or follow-up with a new question or prompt.

Implementation Tip

Resist the urge to call on students to share. Instead, allow the group to control the pace and direction of the conversation.

Examples

- A fourth-grade teacher used *Up and Down* to encourage students to pay attention to the views, values, and beliefs of their peers during a lesson on bullying and peer pressure. More than half of the students in the classroom stood to share experiences they had with bullying and some of the ways they have coped with the struggles related to peer pressure. Six students who did not stand then commented on the contributions from their peers; some of the listeners paraphrased what they heard, and some offered kind words to those who had shared difficult stories.

- In a middle school English class, several students studying the book *Pay It Forward* stood up to respond to the prompt, "Is it practical/possible for young people to pay it forward in meaningful or powerful ways? How?" Only six students stood and answered the question, but 14 responded to the comments shared by those who stood to respond (e.g., "I like what Bella said about the difference between service and good deeds"). A student with learning disabilities in this classroom with an IEP goal of "providing a cogent and appropriate verbal response to content-related questions" was provided with an index card with the same verbal prompts the teacher planned to give in the context of the lesson. He wrote responses on this card before the game began and used it as a guide when he shared his idea verbally.

Do you believe a young person can "pay it forward" in a meaningful way?

_____

_____

_____

_____

If so, what is one way a young person can "pay it forward"?

_____

_____

_____

_____

Methods to Maximize Engagement and Participation

- Have students practice the format using short responses before having them use *Up and Down* on more complex prompts. So you might ask them to share science-themed movies or documentaries they would recommend to others before getting them to respond to a specific question about Kris Koenig's information-packed documentary *400 Years of the Telescope*.

- If you have students who would find it challenging to generate an answer on the spot, provide them with cue cards containing the question you will be asking or the question and a framed paragraph that will help them compose an answer.

- Remind students that both types of responses are valued in this activity. Impress upon them that sharing is not more valuable than paraphrasing or commenting. If some students tend to take on one role more than another, you may want to give them some encouragement or support to try the other.

- Consider teaching words and phrases that will help your students learn appropriate skills of discourse. Phrases that can be used to paraphrase or clarify include the following:
  - I'm not quite sure I understand what _____ is saying. Can you clarify, _____?
  - When_____ said, I think he meant _____. Is that what you meant, _____?
  - I totally agree with _____about _____ because _____.
  - I think _____ made an excellent point about _____.
  - It seems that a lot of us feel that _____.

IDEAS FOR USING THIS STRUCTURE ✏️

AFTER USING THIS STRUCTURE

Did students learn what I intended? Were all students engaged? What changes might be needed to maximize engagement and participation for specific students? How can other team members be involved in co-teaching or instructional support?

All Together Now!

When teachers want to elicit information from the group, they usually need to rely on asking one student at a time for an answer or for feedback. Although this strategy is sometimes quite appropriate, it can be limiting in that it keeps a few students actively engaged (and usually the same few students day after day) and leaves others to day-dream or otherwise potentially disconnect from class. To avoid this common pitfall, try some version of *All Together Now*, a strategy that involves asking for a response from all of your students at once.

Directions

- Ask a question or seek a response of some kind from the group.

- Let students know that you want them to respond in a new way. Tell them that instead of raising hands, you will be asking for another indication that they know the answer.

- This structure can take many forms, as students can be asked to respond using different methods and materials in different situations. Students can:

  o Use mini-chalkboards or mini-whiteboards.
  o Raise fingers, arms, or even feet (e.g., "Hold up three fingers if you agree, two if you don't, and one if you are not sure"; "Raise both of your arms if you feel strongly about what I said and only one if you do not").
  o Use movement and activity (e.g., "Walk to the front of the room if you can answer my question and to the back if you cannot").
  o Hold premade cards (e.g., students have cards with different fractions written on them and hold them up as the teacher shows images of different graphs).
  o Use a whole-class response app such as Formative (www.goformative.com). This particular app allows teachers to create an online assignment or pose a question that students can answer in real time from any device. Students can type, show their work with drawings, or submit images. Results can be displayed for the whole class or privately for the teacher.

Examples

- A kindergarten teacher used *All Together Now* to introduce addition and subtraction to his students. He gave each student two laminated cards—one that represented addition (+) and one that represented subtraction (−). Using two frog puppets and some apples, he performed different scenes in which the frogs either lost apples or found them. After each scene, he asked students to indicate whether the scene involved addition or subtraction. Students, all at once, were required to hold up either their addition card or their subtraction card.

- A high school physics teacher gave students mini-whiteboards and asked a series of questions during a demonstration on momentum. He set up a ramp and rolled different-sized soup cans down it several times, each time making the ramp more or less steep. Using the boards, students were asked to make predictions throughout the demonstration (e.g., the can will roll faster).

- Using the app Formative (www.goformative.com), a health teacher gave students an informal quiz before starting their mini-unit on mental health. Primarily, the teacher asked for single-word and short-phrase responses to questions (e.g., "What is one sign or symptom of depression?"), but she also asked students to occasionally draw a response (e.g., "Draw one thing you do to relieve stress").

Methods to Maximize Engagement and Participation

- It may be particularly helpful in this structure to consciously engineer and monitor the "think time" given to the students. A downfall of most large-group question-and-answer formats is that teachers ask for an answer in fewer than 10 seconds. Consequently, only the students who process verbal language quickly are able to respond. Try setting a timer and allowing at least 15 to 30 seconds for students to develop answers—especially if the prompts are open-ended. If you make this wait time routine, you can assign a student to be the timekeeper.

- Give students the opportunity to compare their individual ideas with a partner and construct their response as a team. This process can decrease anxiety and increase confidence in the choral response.

- Provide a "tips page" filled with key words, phrases, and facts to help students recall material. It can be made available to all students, or it can be given to specific students who need extra support during *All Together Now*. This page can be reviewed before any questions are posed to the large group.

- Some students might be well suited to pose the questions to the large group or demonstrate the problem to be solved. As in the aforementioned physics example, two students could demonstrate the elements of momentum using the ramp and soup cans.

IDEAS FOR USING THIS STRUCTURE

_____
_____
_____
_____
_____
_____
_____
_____
_____
_____
_____
_____
_____
_____
_____
_____

AFTER USING THIS STRUCTURE

Did students learn what I intended? Were all students engaged? What changes might be needed to maximize engagement and participation for specific students? How can other team members be involved in co-teaching or instructional support?

_____
_____
_____
_____
_____
_____
_____
_____
_____
_____
_____
_____
_____
_____

Share and Compare

This structure requires students to work both independently and interdependently. *Share and Compare* is a quick support strategy that gives learners opportunities to check their note-taking abilities by collaborating with a peer. This technique can help students improve their note-taking skills and monitor whether they are able to identify the most critical ideas and details in the day's material.

It's important to remember that the purpose of this exercise is not to have students give their notes to one another, but instead to work cooperatively to fill gaps in their collective understanding of the information.

Directions

- This structure should be used in conjunction with a traditional lecture or whole-class discussion. Begin by asking students to take notes using their preferred style, materials, and format.

- Start your lecture or discussion.

- Stop your lecture or discussion after approximately 10 to 15 minutes. Then, put learners into pairs (or have them work with a student sitting near them) and direct them to "share and compare" notes, focusing on summarizing information and locating misconceptions. Students can also generate questions or solve a problem posed by the instructor.

- After giving the group a few minutes to interact, continue with the lecture or discussion.

- After another 10 to 15 minutes ask learners to "share and compare" notes with the same partner or with a new partner.

- Repeat this pattern of activity until you have completed the lecture or discussion.

Example

- A high school trigonometry teacher used *Share and Compare* as students took notes on applying the trigonometric formulas for finding the areas of triangles, circular sectors, and segments. Because the material was new to all of the students and some were clearly struggling to understand it, he stopped the lecture every 10 minutes and asked students to share and compare notes. He asked them to pay particular attention to the accuracy of the information they were sharing and discussing. As students worked together to improve their notes, he walked from dyad to dyad to answer questions and clarify concepts.

Methods to Maximize Engagement and Participation

- Not all learners need to start from a blank page when taking notes—for instance, English learners or students with certain learning disabilities, intellectual disabilities, and physical disabilities could be provided a set of guided notes to keep them on target during the lecture and to ensure that they will have accurate information to share. A web resource that can be used to create guided notes is www.interventioncentral.org/rti2/guided_notes.

If a student cannot participate using guided notes, the teacher can provide a completed set of notes and require him or her to participate in note-taking by highlighting key words or ideas and putting icons or other markings next to possible discussion items.

- Introduce Google Docs or apps such as Evernote by Evernote or Good Reader by Good.iWare to allow students to take notes using different tools. You may even want to have students choose a tool to use and let them "share and compare" with those using the same or different tools.

- Use *Share and Compare* to teach new note-taking methods. For instance, you might introduce Cornell notes, mind mapping, or outlining during this structure.

- To make this exercise more challenging for some, identify students who typically take detailed, accurate, and complex notes and ask them to reteach a part of the lecture to the group.

IDEAS FOR USING THIS STRUCTURE ✎

_____
_____
_____
_____
_____
_____
_____
_____
_____
_____
_____
_____
_____
_____
_____
_____
_____

AFTER USING THIS STRUCTURE

Did students learn what I intended? Were all students engaged? What changes might be needed to maximize engagement and participation for specific students? How can other team members be involved in co-teaching or instructional support?

_____
_____
_____
_____
_____
_____
_____
_____
_____
_____
_____
_____
_____
_____

Stand and Deliver

Do you want to increase participation in large-group discussions? This technique offers another alternative to the traditional whole-class question-and-answer format, and it can help you get 100 percent of your students focused, engaged, and on their feet (literally).

Often, confident, outspoken students are the first to offer their thoughts in a class discussion. Because teachers want to honor effort and enthusiasm, they often call on these students first. *Stand and Deliver* disrupts this pattern and allows every student to have his or her ideas represented and heard.

This structure promotes active listening because students must be attentive to determine if their responses are the same or different from those offered by others. It also promotes higher-level thinking, as students must make comparisons between their own answers and those presented by classmates.

Benefits for the teacher in using this structure are that she or he can easily see which students have the same ideas and which are the most popular or prevalent answers. In addition, misconceptions can be quickly identified and remedied during *Stand and Deliver.*

Directions

- Pose a question to the group. The question must have a number of viable answers or solutions (e.g., "Suggest one way you could help combat racism, sexism, or ableism in this school").

- Provide parameters for their responses. For instance, you might ask them to provide an answer in "no more than seven words."

- Give the group a few minutes to generate answers.

- Then, direct students to stand.

- Call on one student at a time to share a response. When that answer is given, everyone who shares this answer should sit down (including the person called on by the teacher).

- Then, call on a second student to share a response and be seated. Those who are still standing must again determine if their answer is the same or similar enough to that response to take a seat.

- Repeat the process until no one is left standing.

Implementation Tip

Stand and Deliver pairs well with other structures featured in this book. Try it with *Popcorn, Dinner Party, Moving to the Music,* or *Hot Seat.* After mingling to exchange questions and answers in any one of these structures, ask students to select one idea they heard that was particularly interesting or challenging and have them share that idea during a round of *Stand and Deliver.*

Example

- During a seventh-grade lesson on sexism in fairy tales, students were asked to think of a story they had been told or had read that represented women as evil characters. Students were paired up and given time to discuss their ideas. Cayden, a student who has intellectual disabilities and uses augmentative and alternative communication (AAC) to communicate, was provided actual books to examine and use to convey his answer to a peer. The peer recorded Cayden's answer on his communication system so it could be shared with the class. To make sure that Cayden had practice using his device in the context of standards-based instruction, the teacher called on him first to make sure he was able to share an idea and not just sit as a response to someone else's answer.

  This exercise gave the teacher a measure of which fairy tales were familiar to her class. After listing the class answers, the teacher asked students to further analyze the types of evil women who were represented (e.g., stepmothers, sisters, old women, women who have magical powers).

Methods to Maximize Engagement and Participation

- Students can be put into groups and given time to discuss answers or opinions. Then, when they stand, each person can represent a different viewpoint (not his or her own) that was discussed.

- A student who may not be able to make a reliable assessment about whether her or his own answer is sufficiently different from those offered might be called on first so that an assessment of classmates' responses is unnecessary. This suggestion may also be helpful for students who might sit down immediately to avoid participation.

- Students can work in pairs or small groups to produce a single answer and can sit down together to respond; this speeds up the process and gives students opportunities to learn how to collaborate and synthesize ideas.

- When individual accountability is a concern, ask students to provide a written response to the question or problem before standing to play *Stand and Deliver*. This way, it's possible to verify that a response was formulated by each student and, if needed, the responses can be used as exit tickets for particular lessons.

IDEAS FOR USING THIS STRUCTURE ✎

_____

_____

_____

_____

_____

_____

_____

_____

_____

_____

_____

_____

_____

_____

_____

_____

_____

_____

_____

AFTER USING THIS STRUCTURE

Did students learn what I intended? Were all students engaged? What changes might be needed to maximize engagement and participation for specific students? How can other team members be involved in co-teaching or instructional support?

_____

_____

_____

_____

_____

_____

_____

_____

_____

_____

_____

_____

_____

_____

_____

Chants and Rants

To begin a lesson, to reinforce a concept, or simply to get students more involved in whole-class learning, try the effective and amusing *Chants and Rants*. Asking students to repeat significant phrases, words, or ideas certainly increases engagement, but using chants or other types of call-and-response techniques has the additional benefit of improving learners' chances of remembering the material long after the lesson is over.

Directions

- When designing a lecture, choose words, core concepts, ideas, or a phrase that you want students to remember.

- Then, develop a memorable way to repeat, sing, or chant this information. Consider how you can connect it with well-known past or present songs, spoken word and rap lyrics, or the latest viral video.

- Next, identify potential points in the lecture to interject the chant. A routine chant might be used at the beginning of a class session to reinforce behavioral expectations or raise the energy level of the group. Other chants can be used in the context of the lecture to reinforce content and cue students about which pieces of information are the most important to remember.

- Chants are most effective when they can be used repeatedly over time. Concepts that occur in several contexts or are foundations for other skills are good choices for chants.

Implementation Tip

Although teachers may be most familiar with chants that rhyme (e.g., "Thirty days hath September, April, June, and November . . ."), content doesn't need to be poetic or presented in singsong fashion to be memorable. Just asking students to verbally repeat important information (and use gestures or physical movements, if appropriate) can be a powerful learning strategy. *Chants and Rants* can be used daily and without much or any planning.

Examples

- A high school physics teacher asked his students to chant facts such as "fission *and* fusion release energy" during lectures. It was not uncommon for former students to approach him on the street (even years after they had taken his class) and recite classroom chants.

- A teacher in a fifth-grade classroom used this chant to set behavioral expectations before the start of some lessons or when classroom management needed to be checked. To the tune of "Respect"(the classic song by Aretha Franklin), he would chant the lead vocal, change a few words, and have the students respond as backup singers:

Teacher:	R-E-S-P-E-C-T . . . that is what YOU need for ME!
Teacher:	R-E-S-P-E-C-T. Find out what it means to me.
Teacher:	Oh!
Students:	Sock it to me, sock it to me, sock it to me, sock it to me
Teacher:	A little respect
Students:	Sock it to me, sock it to me, sock it to me, sock it to me
Teacher:	Whoa, babe
Students:	Just a little bit
Teacher:	A little respect
Students:	Just a little bit
Teacher:	I get tired
Students:	Just a little bit
Teacher:	Keep on tryin'
Students:	Just a little bit
Teacher:	You're runnin' out of foolin'
Students:	Just a little bit
Teacher:	And I ain't lyin'
Students:	Just a little bit
All:	(re, re, re, re) 'spect

In most instances, this was enough to set the tone or alter the classroom climate. Sometimes, the teacher would follow the chant by asking students to shout out what respect should look like and sound like in their classroom.

- A middle school English teacher wrote the following chant (to the tune of "Yankee Doodle") for his students during a unit on the Harlem Renaissance:

Langston Hughes was a poet.

He wrote novels and stories too.

Part of the Harlem Renaissance,

his fame just grew and grew.

Students chanted the poem during parts of the teacher's lecture on famous figures of the movement. At the end of the lecture, students were asked to construct their own rap or song on any individual connected to the Harlem Renaissance.

- During a lecture on geometry vocabulary, two coteaching partners (a general education math teacher and a special education teacher) asked their students to do a call-and-response exercise with the following text. Initially, the teachers modeled the chant with one taking the role of the students and one taking the role of the teachers. Then, they asked students to join in:

All:	Talking about angles!
Teachers:	Angles.
Students:	Angles.
All:	Please define . . .
Teachers:	An angle is formed . . .
Students:	An angle is formed . . .
Teachers:	When two rays have the same endpoint.
Students:	When two rays have the same endpoint.
Teachers:	How many rays?
Students:	Two rays.
Teachers:	What is the endpoint called, I ask?
Students:	Vertex.
All:	The common endpoint is the vertex.
Teachers:	Vertex?
Students:	Vertex!
Teachers:	One ray forms the initial side.
Students:	The initial side.
Teachers:	One ray is the terminal side.
Students:	The terminal side.
All:	Talking about angles!

Students were invited to stand and move around during the exercise and eventually to write their own verses related to geometry concepts. Several students with learning disabilities in this class found that this technique helped them to stay attentive during lectures and retain the information the team was teaching. To differentiate the materials, the special and general education math teachers wrote down the words and video recorded the class during the chant so students could study the concepts by watching the video, listening to the words, or singing it themselves.

Methods to Maximize Engagement and Participation

- Project the chant on the interactive whiteboard so students can follow along.

- Give students who may need extra assistance a copy of the chant with their part highlighted in a bright color.

- When appropriate, pair the chant with movements or motions. For instance, if you are using chanting to help students learn Spanish verbs, they can both say the words and act them out.

- Allow students to participate in crafting the chants when possible; you might give them a familiar rhyme or melody to use as a starting point. Audio record the chants so you can play them back as a review exercise. Let students have fun by recording them using apps such as Talking Tom or Talking Ben the Dog, both by Outfit 7 Limited. These apps will not only inspire a lot of laughter, but they will give students a reason to read and hear the chants over and over again.

- Video record the class engaged in *Chants and Rants* so you can play these clips during lectures or right before test time. A student who is very shy or otherwise reluctant to participate might be given the job of recording the class as they chant.

- Young children are typically quite willing to join in on chanting exercises. It is common, for instance, for a teacher to ask elementary-aged students to chant certain number patterns in unison; this is how many of us learned to count by 2s or by 10s. Older students may be more reluctant to participate, but their interest may be piqued if the strategy is introduced as a rap or simply as a useful memory strategy rather than as a chant or rhyme.

IDEAS FOR USING THIS STRUCTURE ✏

AFTER USING THIS STRUCTURE

Did students learn what I intended? Were all students engaged? What changes might be needed to maximize engagement and participation for specific students? How can other team members be involved in co-teaching or instructional support?

 **The Whip**

The purpose of this activity is to increase the number of students who speak up in whole-class discussions, give students practice in self-management, and provide communication practice to those who need it. For these reasons, *The Whip* (Harmin, 1994; Harmin & Toth, 2006) may be an especially attractive structure for teachers who have many students with communication-related disabilities or some who are learning English.

This structure can be used with all or part of the class. In other words, the teacher can "whip around" the entire classroom, or he or she can choose to get a sampling of student ideas by using this structure down one row of the classroom or with just one small group.

Directions

- Announce a topic or question and tell students to generate a response to it. Several different types of prompts can be used for this activity, including these:
    - Sentence starters (e.g., "I think good grammar is important because _____." "An ethical scientist always _____").
    - Open-ended questions (e.g., "How do you think Hitler was able to get Germans to cooperate with his plan?" and "What is one good way to prepare for a test?")
    - Fact-based questions (e.g., "What is one state capital?", "What is 100 divisible by?", "What is one healthy food?", or "Give an example of a simile").

- After giving the group a few moments to think of answers, point to an individual student (usually one sitting in the front or back of a row) and ask for a response.

- After getting a response from the first student, continue down the row (or through a section of the room) and, one by one, ask each student to share an answer.

- Encourage students who cannot think of an answer or those who get frustrated when their answer is used by a classmate to simply repeat another student's answer.

- Engage in this process until you have heard several different answers. Alternatively, you can continue eliciting responses until you have heard from every student in the classroom.

Implementation Tip

If you want to use this structure when you are short on time, consider giving students some parameters to use when constructing their responses. For instance, you can tell them that they each have 15 seconds or only seven words to express an idea or give their answer.

Examples

- A second-grade teacher ended a lesson on the characteristics of living things with *The Whip*. She "whipped" around the entire room, asking each student to name one living thing. A student with learning disabilities was prompted to open her interactive science notebook and review her drawings and notes before playing the game.

- A third-grade teacher started a lesson on estimation by asking all students to name a time when they estimated something.

- A high school physical education teacher used *The Whip* to review a unit on football. He did a quick whip with a handful of students, asking them to complete the sentence, "One rule of football we learned is _____."

- A middle school choral music teacher had all of her students watch a video of the group's most recent performance and asked them to answer the question "How did we do?" in no more than six words.

Methods to Maximize Engagement and Participation

- Let some or all students use flashcards or mini-whiteboards to share a written response.

- Preteach the content to learners who need it; give suggestions for content they might share.

- Give students the option of passing when their turn comes.

- Remind all students that repeating an answer is not only okay, but may also be helpful to the group because students are likely to remember content, ideas, and concepts that they hear several times.

- Start the whip with students who may have difficulty assessing if an answer has been given or may have a limited repertoire of answers.

- Whip around the classroom several times so students needing repeated practice in sharing ideas aloud can get it and so that all learners can hear important information shared from different perspectives and voices.

IDEAS FOR USING THIS STRUCTURE ✎

AFTER USING THIS STRUCTURE

Did students learn what I intended? Were all students engaged? What changes might be needed to maximize engagement and participation for specific students? How can other team members be involved in co-teaching or instructional support?

Numbered Heads Together

It can be a challenge to hear from all students during whole-class instruction. One solution to this problem is to occasionally use small-group discussions to cover the same topics, ideas, or questions. Even in small groups, however, some voices may be quiet or silent. In fact, it is not uncommon to see that the students who lead the discussions in large groups tend to be the same individuals who do so in smaller groups.

Numbered Heads Together, a structure developed and popularized by Spencer Kagan (1992), is one way to encourage participation by all, solicit responses from a greater range of students, and give everyone an equal chance to be an expert.

Directions

- Arrange students in teams of three or four and assign each individual a number (e.g., Pete is *1,* Yolanda is *2,* Amir is *3,* Allison is *4*).

- Assign the groups a question to answer, an idea to brainstorm, or a task to complete—for example, you might ask students to name everything they know about ancient Rome or to generate a list of conductors and semiconductors.

- Give the groups a set time to answer the question and to make sure that everyone can answer the question. Explain that all students are responsible for the learning of all others. Therefore, Pete is not only responsible for providing an answer to the question, but he also needs to make sure that Amir, Yolanda, and Allison can answer the question. Encourage everyone to participate and contribute.

- After giving teams some time to work, ask the question again and call out a student number (e.g., "Tell me what you already know about ancient Rome. I want to hear answers from all of the 4s").

- The student that was assigned that particular number should stand; he or she is responsible for reporting to peers and the teacher.

- Finally, ask the selected students to report to the large group.

Implementation Tip

Consider forming *Numbered Heads* groups early in the school year and keeping students in these groups year round. This way, you can quickly move into the structure during a lecture or discussion without having students count off or get acquainted with those in the group. When students enter the classroom on a given day, you can inform them they will be using *Numbered Heads Together* and invite them to choose or structure their desks accordingly. This ongoing use of the structure will be especially powerful in inclusive classrooms, as you will want students to understand that they will be regularly supporting and teaching each other and working collaboratively.

Example

- A middle school music teacher put students into a *Numbered Heads Together* formation for the last 15 minutes of the day every Friday. The groups remained the same all year (so students never forgot which partners they needed to find or where in the classroom they needed to be), but the questions changed weekly. Sometimes, the teacher would ask questions about curriculum, such as "What are some characteristics of classical music that you can describe using the new terminology we have been learning?" Other times, the questions were aimed at helping students get to know one another better and work together more effectively. For instance, at the beginning of the year, the teacher asked "How can our group work together more effectively?"

Methods to Maximize Engagement and Participation

- Call on two students to answer together (e.g., "I want 2s and 4s to collaboratively give a response").

- If a particular student would have a difficult time sharing in a large-group format, have students write a collective response or responses on paper and give it to that student to hold up or hand to the teacher.

- If a class member uses augmentative or alternative communication (AAC) such as a TalkTablet by Gus Communication Devices, Proloqu02Go by Assistive-Ware, or MyTalkTools by Second Half Enterprises, allow sufficient time for his or her group to record or prepare an answer on the student's system. Then, when a number is called, any student in the group, including those without disabilities, can answer using the AAC system.

- If some students are dominating discussions in this format, provide additional rules, such as "Everyone must speak once before anyone speaks twice." To make this part of the process more concrete, distribute sticks, pebbles, or other participation markers to help students keep track of their contributions to the conversation. Give each student one or two markers and direct them to contribute one to a common pile each time he or she makes a remark. When a student's markers are gone, he or she must wait until others dispense of their markers to make another contribution to the discussion.

IDEAS FOR USING THIS STRUCTURE ✎

AFTER USING THIS STRUCTURE

Did students learn what I intended? Were all students engaged? What changes might be needed to maximize engagement and participation for specific students? How can other team members be involved in co-teaching or instructional support?

©iStockphoto.com/alexjuve

Take My Perspective, Please!

This interactive exercise promotes a number of important skills, including developing a position statement or response to a question, using attentive listening, learning how to paraphrase, having individual accountability, and understanding perspective-taking. *Take My Perspective, Please!* encourages the participation of every student in the classroom and can be used at the beginning of a lesson to generate interest in the subject matter, at the middle of the lesson to check for understanding, or at the end of the lesson to reinforce key learning points.

Directions

- Provide a note card to all students and direct them to write their names anywhere on the card.

- Then, provide a question or prompt that relates to the subject or topic of concern. The best prompts for this activity should be those that have several correct answers or encourage diverse positions, such as these:
  o What is an example of heroism?
  o Consider the rule of the first female pharaoh. Why do you think we have not yet had a female president in the history of the United States?
  o We've learned about successful experiments with animal cloning. What is your position on human cloning?

- Allow students time to formulate an answer to the prompt. Encourage them to write thoughtful and cogent responses, but emphasize that full sentences do not need to be used.

- Then, cue students to stand up, move to a new location in the room, and find a partner. With note card in hand, partners should exchange ideas verbally. Alert students that they should listen attentively and paraphrase what has been said because they will—at some point in the activity—need to represent their partner's ideas.

- After sufficient time is given to swap ideas, tell students to exchange note cards and "take the perspective" of their partners. After this exchange, cue students to find another partner and repeat the exercise. However, this time they must assume the identity of their previous partner and represent that perspective.

- Have them repeat the process several times.

- On returning to a large-group arrangement, ask a few individual students to share the perspectives they have assumed. At this time, be sure to check with the originators of the perspectives to determine if the information was passed along accurately.

Implementation Tips

- Younger students will find it more challenging to retain detailed information across repeated exchanges. When first teaching this structure, it may be necessary to start with an exchange of simple information (e.g., "My favorite winter activity is . . .") and reduce the rounds of exchanges to one or two.

- This structure can be an effective vehicle for older students to examine controversial issues while learning to listen respectfully to a variety of perspectives that differ from their own. To listen to another's perspective is one skill, but to "take on" someone else's perspective and share it out loud without conveying judgment is a much more sophisticated skill. There may be appropriate times for students to develop and share belief statements related to topics such as gun control, immigration law, legalization of marijuana, assisted suicide, or rights of transgender students. Before opening up discussion about topics of this nature, ensure that a solid sense of community has been established in the classroom and that respectful interactions have been taught and are observed.

Examples

- A math teacher used *Take My Perspective, Please!* to encourage students to consider diverse approaches to problem solving. Students were provided a graph representing linear equations related to the increase or decrease of male and female doctors over a 40-year period. Questions drawn from the school's math curriculum materials were posed at different points in the activity and included the following:

  o How would you describe the trends shown in the data points and the linear models that have been drawn to match patterns in those points?

  o How long will the percentage of male doctors remain greater than the percentage of female doctors?

  o If you were asked to make a report on future prospects for numbers of male and female doctors, what kinds of questions could you answer using the linear models? (Core-Plus Mathematics Project, 2005)

  Students were given some time to study the graphs and formulate their own responses before engaging in the idea exchange. Afterward, the math teacher asked the students to analyze and, if appropriate, graph the patterns in responses they heard.

- A high school English teacher used this activity as a way for students to share their thesis statements before writing a five-paragraph essay. Students were given this prompt: What is the most important lesson you think students in our school community need to learn? Students wrote their initial ideas for thesis statements on note cards and then engaged in *Take My Perspective Please!* The teacher provided an additional requirement for students to write an idea on the back of the card that elaborated on their partner's thesis statement before moving on to a new exchange. Students not only heard many original thesis statements but also had new ideas from classmates for their next phase of writing when they received their cards back at the end of the activity.

Methods to Maximize Engagement and Participation

- Let students generate the relevant question to ask based on a reading or short introduction of the subject by the teacher.

- Midway through the session, change or expand the question.

- Some students with language, communication, or processing difficulties may find it problematic to spontaneously generate a response. Be sure to provide adequate "think time" for all students to develop a response.

- The note card with a classmate's ideas on it serves as a built-in "cheat sheet" for partners to remember the new perspective. However, this task still may be too challenging for particular students. Therefore, you may want to allow some students to keep their own position throughout the session. The repetition of the same statement may help build confidence and promote the student's ability to elaborate on the topic.

- A useful piece of assistive technology for students who are nonverbal or simply need a reminder of the concepts they will share is the Step-by-Step voice output device (see Figure 4.1). This device could be used to record and share the student's initial position in the first round, and then, he or she can record each new partner's statement on the device to share in the following round. There are 75 seconds of recording time. Each touch of the switch plays and advances messages in sequence. There is also a message-repeat feature to replay one message in the series.

Figure 4.1 Step-by-Step Communicator

Source: Image courtesy of AbleNet, Inc.

IDEAS FOR USING THIS STRUCTURE

AFTER USING THIS STRUCTURE

Did students learn what I intended? Were all students engaged? What changes might be needed to maximize engagement and participation for specific students? How can other team members be involved in co-teaching or instructional support?

Lecture Reflections

Do your students find it difficult to maintain attention during longer lectures? If so, you may need to add a reflection or two. *Lecture Reflections* is a tool that teachers can use to break up the monotony of a long presentation and boost comprehension of the material at the same time. This structure involves building regular stopping points into lectures and discussions so that students can reflect on and react to the information that has been shared. Responding to a number of sentence starters can help students relate the content immediately to their background knowledge and provide a quick check of understanding. Further, the nature of student responses can provide a signal to reteach content, move forward in the curriculum, or make clarifications.

Directions

- During the preparation of a lecture, identify several logical stopping points suitable for reflection. A general rule to follow is to intersperse such a break every 10 to 15 minutes.

- Before the lecture begins, tell the students that there will be several breaks or stopping points in the lecture; let them know that they will be reflecting and writing short responses at these times. At the stopping points, provide a prompt and allow sufficient time for students to write a brief response to it. Then, begin the lecture again.

- Repeat the process. Students can continue to write additional reflections on the same paper, on separate sheets, or on a tablet or laptop.

- At some stopping points, ask several students to share their reflections aloud.

- After the lecture, collect and review the responses. Student work may reveal misunderstandings or insights that provide direction for instruction in the next day's lesson.

- A number of potential sentence starters for reflections follow:
    o I think . . .
    o I wonder . . .
    o What's hard about this is . . .
    o What puzzles me is . . .
    o I am unsure about . . .
    o What's interesting is . . .
    o One area that I need further practice in is . . .
    o A strength for me is . . .
    o Something I need to work harder on is . . .
    o It was great when . . .
    o I was surprised that . . .
    o I already knew about . . . but learned that . . .
    o Others say _____ about (the topic) . . .
    o I learned . . .
    o It's okay that . . .
    o I am concerned that . . .

- o I am affirmed when . . .
- o I feel secure when . . .
- o I think what will happen is . . .
- o This is different because . . .
- o I feel confident about . . .
- o It made me think of . . .
- o I could visualize . . .
- o I figured out . . .

Implementation Tip

It's very helpful to share the purpose for using this active lecture technique with your students, as some may be puzzled about the change in the pace and rhythm of the classroom. Letting them in on the rationale for this type of instruction can give them insight into their own learning and may, consequently, motivate them to participate and give them an idea to use when they are studying on their own or designing instruction for their peers (e.g., science fair, class presentations).

Example

- During an introductory science lecture for sixth graders on the topic of plate tectonics and the earth's structure, the instructor presented the following set of reflections for the purpose of checking student understanding and background knowledge:
  - o A concept that kind of confused me was . . .
  - o I already knew about . . . but learned . . .
  - o Tomorrow, I'd like you to review . . .
  - o I could visualize . . .

  In this bilingual classroom, there were a number of English learners, so the instructor projected the sentences on the interactive whiteboard in both English and Spanish. Students could also look to the screen to view a set of vocabulary words in both languages that any student could use to construct a response. Vocabulary words and phrases that could be used to complete the sentence starters included *layers of the Earth, plate boundaries, plate motion, continental drift, seafloor spreading,* and *Pangaea.*

Methods to Maximize Engagement and Participation

- Combine *Lecture Reflections* with other types of breaks or active-lecture techniques (e.g., *Chants and Rants*) to keep the learning process fresh and interesting. Follow the rule not to talk continuously for more than 10 to 20 minutes—that is, about 10 to 15 minutes for elementary or middle school students and about 15 to 20 minutes for high school learners.

- Instead of providing just one option, provide a short list of three or four prompts that students can choose to address or answer.

- For students who are unable to write well spontaneously or who may have difficulty formulating a complete response in the time offered, prepare a number of pretyped responses. These learners can select the response that best fits their ideas and thoughts on the topic and add to or highlight the prepared response. Alternatively, you might create multiple-choice response cards that include key words or pictures. This way, students can circle an answer instead of writing one out (see Figure 4.2 for an example).

- Periodically, allow students to turn and talk to one another after the sentence starter or prompt is given and ask for responses verbally rather than in writing.

- Place pieces of chart paper around the room and record one sentence starter on each. When you stop the lecture, have students get up and write responses on the chart or charts of their choice.

- Allow students to choose the materials they use for their responses. Offer note cards, sketchbooks, tablets or laptops, whiteboards, and even poster paper and markers.

Figure 4.2 *Lecture Reflections* **Response Cards**

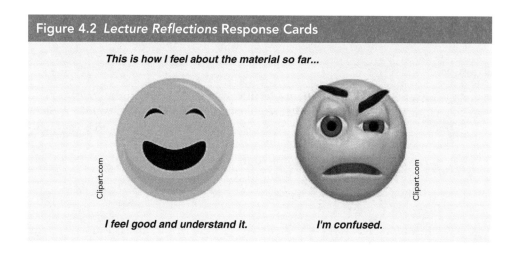

This is how I feel about the material so far...

Clipart.com

Clipart.com

I feel good and understand it.   *I'm confused.*

IDEAS FOR USING THIS STRUCTURE

AFTER USING THIS STRUCTURE

Did students learn what I intended? Were all students engaged? What changes might be needed to maximize engagement and participation for specific students? How can other team members be involved in co-teaching or instructional support?

Stop the Lecture and Start the Drama

To bring out the drama kings and queens in the classroom, assign students to engage in short role plays or skits to demonstrate their understanding of classroom material. These sketches can be a serious rendition of important facts or can be developed as parodies and satires of a situation. These role plays work best to illustrate events, demonstrate roles of critical figures in history, or show the process of a tangible sequence. Props are optional, but encouraged!

Directions

- Before the lecture begins, tell the students that they will be responsible for creating a skit or scenario that represents some aspect of the lecture content. Identify the scenarios in advance so students can be alert to salient points and details in the lecture. To facilitate a smooth transition to the skits, identify the size and members of the role-play groups before beginning the lecture.

- Then, identify stopping points in the lecture where the role plays can be inserted. Choose a few different points to give several groups the chance to take the stage.

- At the planned stopping points, provide the scenario to be represented and invite your group or groups to come forward. Examples of scenarios include the discovery of electricity, Rosa Parks being arrested for refusing to ride in the back of the bus, Japanese families arriving at an internment camp, or primitive man learning to use fire.

- If time permits and your students are game, change your scenes up a bit to make them quirky, funny, or otherwise unique. For instance, twists of humor that force critical comparisons can be fostered by blending current and past viewpoints. Ask teams to role-play an air traffic controller commenting on the first flight of the Wright brothers, make Attila the Hun appear in Judge Judy's court, or place the leaders of two warring countries on the *Dr. Phil* show.

- After the role plays, invite the audience to make comments.

- Conclude by adding relevant teaching points.

Implementation Tip

Incorporate some classic improvisational techniques into the role play for a challenge and to liven up the skit. For example, students could follow some or all of these rules:

- There must be physical contact among all group members at some point.
- Several seconds of slow motion must be included.
- A moment when everyone is looking up must be incorporated.
- One actor must be an inanimate object (e.g., a table, lamp, a chair).
- At least five hand gestures must be integrated.
- Several seconds of silence must be observed at some point.
- Three vocabulary words from the lesson must be used.

Figure 4.3 Strategic Note-Taking Form for Women's Rights Lecture

Name: _____

Fill in this portion before the lecture begins. ✎

What is today's topic?

Describe what you know about the topic:

As the instructor lectures, take the following notes. ✎

List three to seven main ideas from today's lecture/discussion. Include details, if possible.

* _____
* _____
* _____
* _____
* _____
* _____
* _____

Summary—Briefly describe how the ideas or information on women's rights across historical eras are similar or related:

Summary—Briefly describe how the ideas or information on women's rights across historical eras are different:

New Vocabulary or Terms:

* _____   * _____
* _____   * _____
* _____   * _____

Examples

- During a mini-lecture on the space program, different groups of students came forward to perform skits related to the moon landing. Some acted out the first steps on the moon and others performed a skit set at mission control.

- After presenting a comparison of women's rights across eras of history, a world history teacher posed the following scenario: "Imagine Nefertiti, Sojourner Truth, Eleanor Roosevelt, Betty Friedan, and Hillary Clinton getting together for lunch and comparing their rights as women." To facilitate participation of a student with learning disabilities and ensure that all students came to the role play with information to share, the instructor provided a guide for strategic note-taking (Boyle, 2001), as shown in Figure 4.3 (page 141).

Methods to Maximize Engagement and Participation

- To get students comfortable with the look and feel of the skits, give a demonstration. If you coteach with partners (e.g., therapists, general or special educators, administrators), get together and show students how it's done! If you don't have partners in the classroom, this activity might provide inspiration to start a collaboration. If you want your speech therapist, social worker, or reading specialist to work in your general education classroom on a more regular basis, introduce them to the class in this fun and entertaining way.

- If you have students who are not yet ready to be the primary actors in the role play, ensure that they have contributed ideas to the skit and are in charge of some aspect of the presentation (e.g., creating props, participating in a non-speaking role).

- Rather than having one group perform in front of the whole class, arrange small group-to-group demonstrations. This type of performance can be less intimidating to some students. In addition, this format expedites the process and gives students more time to perform.

- Some students might be assigned roles as skit judges (á la *Dancing With the Stars*) and be encouraged to score performances and offer humorous but respectful critiques.

- For students who may have trouble changing roles frequently or acting out ever-changing information, consider the use of role plays that have a consistent character, common introduction, or guided narration.

IDEAS FOR USING THIS STRUCTURE

_____
_____
_____
_____
_____
_____
_____
_____
_____
_____
_____
_____
_____
_____
_____
_____
_____

AFTER USING THIS STRUCTURE

Did students learn what I intended? Were all students engaged? What changes might be needed to maximize engagement and participation for specific students? How can other team members be involved in co-teaching or instructional support?

_____
_____
_____
_____
_____
_____
_____
_____
_____
_____
_____
_____
_____
_____
_____
_____

Roundtable

Roundtable (Kagan, 1992) is a collaborative technique that begins with a blank sheet of paper and ends with the creation of a common product such as a list, a paragraph, or even a picture. Originally designed as a general brainstorming technique, it also can be used for review, as a check for understanding during a lecture, or to focus attention during a movie or video clip.

Directions

- Seat students in groups around a table with a single device or one pencil and one piece of paper.

- Then, pose a question and have students take turns recording answers as the device or paper is passed around the table.

- Choose the question carefully. It should have multiple answers, and all students should be capable of responding to it in some way (e.g., "How did children contribute to and help the war effort during WWI?" or "What strategies do you use for multiplying?").

- When time is called, have teams count their responses.

- Then, ask groups how many responses they collected. In addition, have them evaluate their lists for the most creative or on-target responses.

- Finally, ask each group to summarize their list in a few sentences.

Examples

- A second-grade teacher asked students to answer the question "What makes our community unique?" First, students discussed the question with their group members. Then, they silently passed a sheet around the group, and every child added one or two words related to their discussion.

- As sixth-grade students were watching a documentary on endangered species, the teacher gave tablets to table groups of six students. When the film started, the first student watched until he or she could find a response to the question "What is one thing you learned about endangered species?" Then, he or she recorded a response and passed it to the next student. When that student was able to answer the question, he or she jotted a response and continued to pass the tablet. When the sixth student in the group added an answer, he or she passed the tablet back to the first student to begin the process anew. Students took turns in this way until the film ended.

- During a mini-lecture by the tenth-grade family and consumer education teacher about child development, each table of students was given a sheet of paper to collectively write a set of notes. As the instructor presented the lesson, one student in the group wrote down an important point and then passed the paper to the student sitting to his or her right. This process of passing the paper around the group continued for the entire mini-lecture. The notes were then reviewed with the teacher for accuracy and duplicated for the class. A student on the autism spectrum in this class was not always able to select the most salient information from the teacher's lecture during his turn. To support his participation, the teacher watched when he received the *Roundtable* paper and emphasized the importance of note-taking at that time. For example, she would pause and say, "This is an important point," and then write it on the whiteboard as a cue for the student to record the information.

- In a high school art class, the instructor transformed an individual assignment into a collective project by using *Roundtable*. Creating a mask out of clay had traditionally been a solo project in the class, with each student making his or her own mask. The teacher, however, wanted students to engage in a collaborative project and decided to change the assignment for this purpose. To use *Roundtable*, she placed students in groups of four and provided one lump of clay to a student on the team. That student made one contribution to the mask (e.g., shaping a nose) and then handed the clay to the next student, who added a second feature before passing it on. The clay "changed hands" throughout the class session, with each person adding a new feature or changing the element that previous teammates had created. This collective method worked well for a student in class with a significant physical disability who could add an undefined feature (e.g., a small lump of clay added for an ear) that would then be refined or embellished by the next person to receive the mask.

Another Version of This Activity

For a "silent discussion," place students in groups of four at tables and give each person a different colored marker. Put a large piece of chart paper in the center of each table. Divide the paper into quadrants. Provide a question about a text, lecture, or video. Then, tell them to write a short response to the question for one minute in their assigned quadrant. At the one-minute mark, have them all rotate their papers to the right so that each person has a new quadrant and can see the response just written by the person next to him or her. Then, give students one minute to react to their classmates' contribution before repeating the process and having them rotate the papers once again.

Methods to Maximize Engagement and Participation

- Allow a student who cannot write or talk to point to an existing response with which he or she agrees. A tally mark can then be placed by that response.

- To provide an alternative to writing, give students stickers containing two or three responses; when they get the page, they can attach one of the stickers to the *Roundtable* paper.

- Give all students the option of adding graphics, highlighting a favorite response, or writing a phrase on the paper.

- Use tablets and laptops for this structure if you have students with fine-motor struggles.

IDEAS FOR USING THIS STRUCTURE

_____
_____
_____
_____
_____
_____
_____
_____
_____
_____
_____
_____
_____
_____
_____
_____
_____

AFTER USING THIS STRUCTURE

Did students learn what I intended? Were all students engaged? What changes might be needed to maximize engagement and participation for specific students? How can other team members be involved in co-teaching or instructional support?

_____
_____
_____
_____
_____
_____
_____
_____
_____
_____
_____
_____
_____
_____
_____
_____

Assessing and Celebrating 5

 ## Question, Comment, and Summarize

Sometimes, you need to break out of your rut and find a new way to pair students for academic conversations. You can certainly use a "turn-and-talk" strategy or simply have students pick a partner sitting near them, but *Question, Comment, and Summarize* is a bit more interesting and gives students practice in developing three important discourse skills: answering questions, commenting, and summarizing.

Directions

- Give each student a *Question, Comment, and Summarize* worksheet as shown in Figure 5.1. Explain that they will need to find one classmate for each of these three roles.

- Have students walk around the classroom, seeking signatures for their forms. Remind them that if they sign a classmate's form on one of the three lines, that person needs to sign her or his form in the same spot.

- When students have completed their forms, start using the structure.

- At some point in classroom lecture or discussion, pose a question to the group and announce, "Time for a question." Students should immediately jump out of their seats, find their question partner, and begin answering the question as a team.

- After a few minutes, direct students to come back to their desks.

- Begin your lecture or discussion again.

- When you get to a point in the lecture or discussion where you want students to make comments and reflect on the material, announce, "Time for a comment." Again, they should leave their seats, pair up, and exchange comments.

- After a few minutes, direct students to come back to their desks.

- Begin your lecture or discussion again.

- When you are nearing the end of the lesson—or at least the discussion portion of it—announce, "Time for a summary," and give students time to find their summary partners and to recap the material that was shared in the lecture.

- End the lesson after students share their summaries, or bring them back to the whole group to debrief.

Implementation Tip

During longer classroom discussions or lectures, give students more than one opportunity to meet with one or more of their partners. You might call for "comment partners" three times during a lesson or give students two different opportunities to answer questions.

Example

- To introduce his fourth-grade students to a unit on entrepreneurship, a teacher showed a few video clips of successful business owners talking about their ideas and their companies. After showing the first clip, he asked students to find their question partners and had them discuss "Why do we need entrepreneurs?" Then, students came back to their seats, and he showed a second clip. After this viewing, students were directed to find their comment partners. This time, they simply shared their thoughts on the two clips, comparing and contrasting the stories of the two featured women. Finally, students returned to their seats to see a third clip. They then met with their summary partners to share all they had learned from both the clips and their discussions.

Methods to Maximize Engagement and Participation

- Practice transitions before the lesson begins. Give learners practice finding their partners and getting back to their seats quickly.

- Try using chimes or another auditory cue to bring students back to their seats after their question, comment, or summarizing "meetings."

- Instead of announcing when it is time to find partners, try holding up or projecting a visual instead (e.g., a speech bubble for comment partners). This breaks up the lesson a bit and can make transitions quicker and easier—especially for those students who are not strong auditory learners.

- If you have a group that needs a little more movement, give them more than one opportunity to answer a question or comment during a lesson.

- Engineer some of the partnerships for your students. If you want to be purposeful with your groupings, hand out partner worksheets with one or more sections already completed. You might let them choose their own summary partners, for instance, but assign their question and comment partners.

- Add other types of partners to this activity. You might have students choose "review partners," for instance. These pairs might assemble at the beginning of the activity to share their thoughts and recollections from a previous day's lesson.

Figure 5.1 *Question, Comment, and Summarize* Worksheet

Question, Comment, and Summarize Partners

Name _____

Directions

- Walk around the classroom and find three different classmates to sign up for the three roles below. When someone signs up to be your partner for one of the roles, you need to sign up for the same role on their sheet.

- Keep this sheet handy so you can easily find your partners when asked to do so.

My Question Partner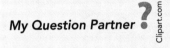

My Comment Partner

My Summary Partner

IDEAS FOR USING THIS STRUCTURE

AFTER USING THIS STRUCTURE

Did students learn what I intended? Were all students engaged? What changes might be needed to maximize engagement and participation for specific students? How can other team members be involved in co-teaching or instructional support?

Countdown

Countdown is a little fast, a little frenetic, and a lot of fun. It gives students the ability to move, talk, share, and interact while providing them with a partner for discussing an issue, completing a task, or participating in an upcoming activity. This structure is particularly handy because it can serve as a flexible grouping strategy, a brain break, and an informal assessment at the same time.

What is the best part of *Countdown?* Students never tire of it because the commands can be changed every time it is played; every game of *Countdown,* therefore, can be completely unique.

Directions

- Have all learners stand to begin the game.

- Then, using your whiteboard, share a list of directions.

- Have students read the list of directions and—on your command—follow them in order. They will follow five different directions in all.

- Be sure to list activities in a countdown format; that is, start with an action that students will complete five times, then have them follow that with an action they will complete four times, and so on. For example, you might ask students to engage in the following actions:

  o   Shake hands with five different people.
  o   Touch all four walls in the room.
  o   Do three jumping jacks.
  o   Walk around two different desks.
  o   Find one partner and discuss/work on/create _____ until time is called.

  The last command should always be related to finding a partner and completing a task. So you might say to students, "Find someone who is standing near you and discuss the questions at the end of Chapter 8," or "Find someone who has the same birthday season you do and create a map of our school together."

Examples

- A middle school math teacher used *Countdown* as a prep strategy for upcoming unit tests. The day before a test, he did a quick whole-class review and then completed two different versions of *Countdown* so that students worked with two different study partners during the last 30 minutes of the class period. The teacher used this as an informal assessment and eavesdropped on students to listen to their questions and answers and fill in any gaps in learning.

- A high school Spanish teacher used this structure as a performance assessment. As students completed each step in the sequence, he observed them and assessed their understanding of the commands (e.g., *"Tocar las cuatro paredes"*). Students had another chance to work on their language skills when they found their partners. At this point, conversation skills were the target behavior. Students were given a topic (e.g., football, dogs, the weather) and were instructed to chat informally about it in Spanish. Students got points for following the directions correctly and for using assigned vocabulary words in their conversations.

Methods to Maximize Engagement and Participation

- Create even more steps and commands for groups that need a longer break and a little more movement. Don't be afraid, for instance, to add commands that take students out of the room or out of the building.

- Be purposeful with your pairings. Choose a final command that puts students into contact with partners you choose. You can do this by giving all of them some sort of visual, such as poker chips, and asking them to find another student with the same color chip they have.

- Model the steps before you have students try them. Some students, such as those who are learning English or are Deaf or hard of hearing, may need a demonstration of toe touches, arm circles, or pirouettes.

- Adapt this for students who have mobility challenges by creating five actions that do not require walking or navigating the entire classroom. Commands such as these will work well for all:
  - "Air spell" five vocabulary words.
  - Touch four neighboring desktops.
  - Roll your neck or shoulders three times.
  - Define two words from the weekly list.
  - Do some "chair dancing" (e.g., the Swim, the Twist) with a partner.

IDEAS FOR USING THIS STRUCTURE

AFTER USING THIS STRUCTURE

Did students learn what I intended? Were all students engaged? What changes might be needed to maximize engagement and participation for specific students? How can other team members be involved in co-teaching or instructional support?

Are You Game?

Most teachers realize that games are motivating and fun for students of any age. They may not understand, however, how much learners can profit from playing and, in this case, creating their own games. Students will surely be excited to engage in this structure, and some may even surprise the teacher by using their creations outside of the classroom and extending their learning beyond the confines of a particular unit.

Directions

- Put learners into pairs or small groups to create a board game that will teach the players about the curriculum being studied. Students might be given anywhere from 30 minutes to several hours to construct their game.

- Provide a range of materials to each group, including paper, poster board, dice, spinners, markers (from other board games in the classroom), and index cards.

- Introduce any rules up front, such as these:
  - The game must have a name related to our course content (e.g., Prime Number Pop Quiz or Fun With Figurative Language).
  - The game must help us learn about _____ (e.g., poetry, integers, world religions, genetics).
  - The game must have simple rules that students in this classroom can easily read and follow.

- Give students time to play their games. If possible, provide time for students to play more than one game.

Implementation Tip

If time is at a premium, have students construct card games instead of board games.

Example

- Students in one sixth-grade class were responsible for creating board games after studying China for several weeks. They were asked to select one piece of the unit to use as the area of focus for the game (e.g., geography, recent history). One team created a game based on China's geography; they called it China: Surrounded by the Seas. Players had to "travel" from Mongolia to the Yellow Sea, the East China Sea, or the South China Sea, answering questions about the 14 border countries of China and the various provinces of the nation as they moved from square to square. The teacher strategically assigned different roles to different students in the groups. One student, Suj, who had an intellectual disability, was working on an individual goal of "locating China on a map." His role was to draw and label a map of Asia on the game board and on the cover of the game box while other students took on the responsibilities of researching questions and designing the board.

Methods to Maximize Engagement and Participation

- Assign students different roles in their groups (e.g., art director, information gatherer) to make sure that everyone participates in a meaningful way.

- Provide examples of different types of games and allow students to review the rules and materials of some of the games that are kept in the classroom.

- If some of your students want an additional challenge, you might allow them to design a computer game or app.

- If some students are struggling to create an original idea (or if time is limited), let them use an existing game board and materials and have them adapt the rules and questions instead of designing a new game.

- You can challenge all or some students by asking them to create a game that could possibly be produced for use by those outside the classroom. Older students, in particular, might be able to create a unique product that could be used across classrooms in the district. Some students may even want to engage in market research or work with a local toy store to further develop their ideas.

IDEAS FOR USING THIS STRUCTURE ✎

_____
_____
_____
_____
_____
_____
_____
_____
_____
_____
_____
_____
_____
_____
_____
_____
_____
_____

AFTER USING THIS STRUCTURE

Did students learn what I intended? Were all students engaged? What changes might be needed to maximize engagement and participation for specific students? How can other team members be involved in co-teaching or instructional support?

_____
_____
_____
_____
_____
_____
_____
_____
_____
_____
_____
_____
_____
_____
_____
_____

Desktop Teaching

Desktop Teaching is an active learning strategy designed to give students the opportunity to act as both teachers and learners (Draper, 1997; Parker, 1990). Students teach one another in a fair-like atmosphere after they have prepared a lesson based on a topic or objective that is assigned to them or that they have chosen. Although this format works very well for formal presentations, such as those commonly associated with science fairs or final assessments, *Desktop Teaching* can also be used more informally to review or reinforce content.

Directions

- Assign topics for *Desktop Teaching,* or provide a list of topics and let students choose their own area of study.

- Provide time for students to develop a short presentation related to their topic. Presentations should be about 5 to 10 minutes long. Encourage students to include visual aids and other learning materials, demonstrations, and short audience-participation activities in their lessons.

- After students complete their presentations, have about half of the students set up materials on their desks for teaching. Have the remaining students choose a "desktop" to visit. Once every student has found one, direct all of the presenters to begin their talks.

- After about 10 minutes, ask students to find a new desktop presentation to attend.

- Repeat this process until students have seen several presentations.

- Then, have the "desktop educators" switch roles. The audience members should set up their presentations, and the presenters should take on the role of audience members.

- Repeat the entire sequence with this group.

Implementation Tip

Take some time to teach the students about good teaching; give them tips for staying within time limits, presenting information in a memorable way, and eliciting participation from their audience. You might even share some of the strategies in this book with your students. If possible, give them time to rehearse their lesson with a partner.

Examples

- Students in a seventh-grade industrial technology class used *Desktop Teaching* as a way to showcase their learning at the end of the year. Each student in the class chose an independent study topic to explore in depth. On their desktop displays, students were required to have at least one model or visual for the presentation and a short handout that their classmates could study and keep.

Desktop lesson topics included tension and compression forces, bridge design, ancient technologies, and computer programming. This hands-on structure, although beneficial for every active learner in the classroom, was very helpful for the eight students in the classroom who were English learners, as these students were able to both hear and see the concepts being studied. Furthermore, they were able to practice conversational English while engaged in academic work.

- During a social studies unit featuring great peacemakers of the world, a fifth-grade teacher asked students to use the Internet to gather information about peacemakers past and present (e.g., Gandhi; Wangari Maathi, the Kenyan environmentalist). Each student was expected to use the information to prepare a short report for *Desktop Teaching*. James, a student with language-based learning disabilities, found it difficult to stay on topic as well as to share the most salient points of a report without providing excessive and sometimes unrelated details. To help keep his desktop presentation succinct and organized, he was assisted by his teacher to construct a picture-based semantic web with Kidspiration Software as he gathered information from the Internet. Using the software, James constructed a visual diagram to organize the main and supporting topics of his presentation on Mahatma Gandhi. The graphic assisted him to organize his thinking about his topics before the presentation and self-monitor the amount of detail he intended to share with his classmates. See Figure 5.2 for an example of a semantic map.

Methods to Maximize Engagement and Participation

- If a student has a special interest, he or she may be encouraged to incorporate it into the presentation—for example, a student who enjoys sports may want to include a game of some sort in his or her lesson.

- Encourage students to teach using their strengths; if a student loves to draw, encourage him or her to use visuals and original art to convey information. If a student is a techie, allow her or him to present using software such as Prezi (www.prezi.com) or SlideDog (www.slidedog.com).

- Give timid students time and space to rehearse their presentations. If you have learners with serious public speaking fears, consider video recording their rehearsals and playing the video during the desktop exchange. The student can play the video for the presentation portion of the lesson but be available for questions and reactions from his or her classmates.

- Presentations themselves can also be video recorded. These can be made available to any student who can benefit from hearing the information repeated several times.

- Encourage learners to develop a theme for their lesson to increase motivation and make the presentation itself memorable. For example, a student in one classroom taught her classmates about the coordinate grid and graphing lines using an "under-the-sea" theme. She made a large, blue coordinate grid to represent the sea, and she had students plot points to represent the fish and lines to represent the seaweed (Draper, 1997).

Figure 5.2 Graphic Organizer of Gandhi Using Kidspiration

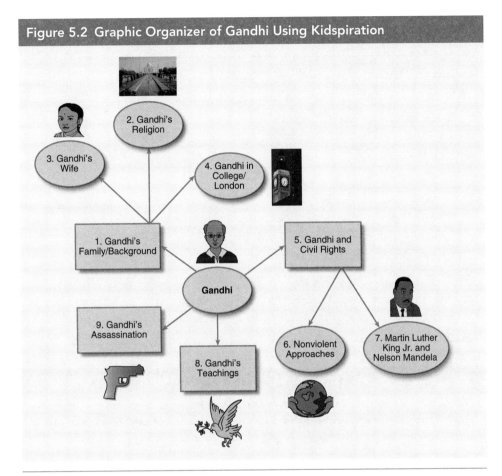

Source: Inspiration Software®, Inc.; Clipart.com.

IDEAS FOR USING THIS STRUCTURE ✎

_____
_____
_____
_____
_____
_____
_____
_____
_____
_____
_____
_____
_____
_____
_____
_____

AFTER USING THIS STRUCTURE

Did students learn what I intended? Were all students engaged? What changes might be needed to maximize engagement and participation for specific students? How can other team members be involved in co-teaching or instructional support?

_____
_____
_____
_____
_____
_____
_____
_____
_____
_____
_____
_____
_____
_____

Gallery Walk

This structure can make an ordinary day in the classroom seem refined and sophisticated! *Gallery Walk* allows students to play the parts of museum visitor and artist and gives them a chance to represent their thoughts visually instead of in words. This structure is an easy and efficient way to summarize learning from a day, month, or year, and it engenders a sense of togetherness and cooperation, as each image is a product of "groupthink."

Directions

- Put students into small groups.

- Provide an idea that can be represented visually. This does not mean that the idea has to be concrete. Sometimes abstract concepts inspire the most interesting visual products.

- Decide on what type of product you want students to produce. You might choose, for instance, an outline, a collage, a map, or a graphic organizer. Ask students to paint a street scene from New York City in 1900, create illustrations for the Native American legend *The Buffalo and the Mouse,* draw the carbon cycle, or create a Venn diagram comparing and contrasting geometry and algebra.

- Give the group a set amount of time to work on their outline, collage, map, or graphic organizer.

- When work time is over, tell the groups to mount their posters somewhere in the classroom, preferably a few feet away from another group's poster.

- Choose one student from each group to stay by the poster in the role of docent as others in the group walk around the classroom or "gallery" and view posters created by other groups. The docent presents the product to those who "visit." She or he should provide a description of the visual and answer any questions from visitors. Visitors should not only examine the posters but also talk to the docent from each group and discuss the gallery products with one another.

Examples

- To complete a unit on simple machines, a science teacher assigned one type of machine to each of six small groups. Students had to create a poster of their machine, including a few drawings and some examples showing how their machine is used in daily life. Students had a class period to create their poster and another period to engage in the gallery walk. During the walk, students brought clipboards and were instructed to take notes on new things they learned. To challenge those who had a more sophisticated understanding of the concepts, the teacher invited local engineers (mostly parents of students in the school) to visit the gallery and exchange ideas with the students. The *Gallery Walk* served as an informal assessment of learning. Students were assessed on the accuracy and detail of their posters, as well as the quality of questions and feedback they provided to others.

- In a high school family and consumer education class, the teacher used this structure to teach the concept of "responsibility." She asked students—in groups of three—to think about the word *responsibility* (as it relates to family, personal growth, and adult life) and discuss ideas they connected to this word. Then, the teacher had each group create a piece of art representing the word. They were given only 20 minutes to create the art (which inspired creativity). They were also given limited materials but were allowed to use anything from their lockers, purses, or pockets (which inspired great variety in the responses). Then, all of the students had an opportunity to travel around the room, examine the creations, and share any observations by creating a video clip testimonial on a laptop that was available near each product. This activity was used as an introduction to all of the year's topics, including work and vocational choices, pregnancy and family planning, personal finance, and independent living.

Methods to Maximize Engagement and Participation

- Depending on the needs and abilities of students, ask class members to take on other specific roles during the observation piece of the activity. A student may serve as a reporter, for instance, and be responsible for interviewing the "gallery patrons"; another may be asked to serve as the gallery photographer so the visual information is captured for future study.

- If some students find it physically challenging to make diagrams or drawings, offer a wider range of tools for constructing and creating. In addition to drawing, students might be given the options of using design software, paints, clay sculpture, or collage materials.

- Rotate the docent role so that no one misses the opportunity to explore and learn from the gallery, or choose individuals who need targeted skill practice and keep them in the role for the entire activity for that purpose. For instance, a middle school student who needs reading fluency practice could practice a script with a teacher and then be asked to share it repeatedly with all who visit his or her poster.

- Do away with docents and let the tech do the talking. Have each group include an audio QR code that describes their poster. Then, during the gallery walk, students can scan the codes to learn about the posters. Go to Smore.com for directions to create an audio QR code (smore.com/4hkp-create-an-audio-qr-code). Additional software tools for making audio QR codes include Record MP3 (recordmp30nline.com), Vocaroo (Vocaroo.com), and QR Stuff (qrstuff.com).

IDEAS FOR USING THIS STRUCTURE

_____
_____
_____
_____
_____
_____
_____
_____
_____
_____
_____
_____
_____
_____
_____
_____
_____
_____
_____

AFTER USING THIS STRUCTURE

Did students learn what I intended? Were all students engaged? What changes might be needed to maximize engagement and participation for specific students? How can other team members be involved in co-teaching or instructional support?

_____
_____
_____
_____
_____
_____
_____
_____
_____
_____
_____
_____
_____
_____
_____
_____

A Is for _____

Take a nostalgic trip back to childhood with this structure. In *A Is for _____*, students engage in a whimsical content review and are asked to show what they know through the familiar structure of an alphabet book. This activity brings a sense of playfulness into the classroom, especially when it is used in upper primary grades, middle school, and high school. It also helps students immerse themselves in content-related websites, books, and notes as they search materials to find words and phrases that correspond with each letter of the alphabet.

Directions

- Tell students that they will be teaching each other class content by creating and sharing alphabet books.

- Provide a range of materials for students to use in their creations. For instance, you might allow the use of presentation software (e.g., PowerPoint), paper and markers, blank books, calligraphy pens, alphabet stickers and stamps, or magazine words and phrases.

- When they finish creating their books (complete with illustrations, of course), have students read them to one another as a way to further reinforce course content.

- Leave the books in the classroom; use them for review and practice at different points during the unit or during the year.

Examples

- Students in an American history class were charged with creating alphabet books to represent different areas of study they had covered during the year. One group, assigned the Harlem Renaissance, created a book with the following pages:
  - A is for African American.
  - B is for black migration.
  - C is for cultural movement.
  - D is for drama.
  - E is for Edward Burra.
  - F is for fiction.

  The books served as assessments and as collaborative teaching tools.

- A high school chemistry teacher used this structure as the format for a semester exam review project that he titled *A Is for Acids, B Is for Bases*. His objective was to help students review conceptual topics taught during the semester. The parameters of the project were to work in partnerships to create a PowerPoint e-book of 26 slides that reviewed the topics of thermodynamics, gases, solutions, and acids and bases. Each slide had to contain a title, two or more pictures with explanations, and a three- to four-sentence description of the slide's topic. Grading criteria included elements related to the technical development of a the presentation, accuracy of information, and creativity.

- During a unit about the sea, students in a first-grade classroom were placed in cooperative groups of three and asked to agree on a sea creature to feature in a book. Each child was assigned one page to write and illustrate. A group that selected dolphins as their topic wrote the following text: "A is for active because dolphins play and swim fast. B is for beautiful because they have shiny and smooth skin. C is for cute because they squeak and have a happy smile." All students in class were given a list of descriptive words starting with an *a*, *b*, or *c* from which to choose and were required to write why they chose that descriptor (e.g., *beautiful* because they have shiny and smooth skin). Alex, a student with significant motor planning and eye-hand coordination difficulty, was a member of the dolphin group. The occupational therapist facilitated this group while also assisting Alex. Alex was able to dictate his ideas verbally but was unable to write or draw, so with the support of the therapist, he typed his response on the computer using an adapted keyboard and selected a picture from Google Images to contribute to the book.

Methods to Maximize Engagement and Participation

- Show students samples of alphabet books. Point out the different styles of art and the different formats of the books. This will help learners get ideas for their book's style and content.

- Brainstorm as a class before constructing the books; have students shout out possible words and phrases for topics you suggest. You may want to have a student, a paraprofessional, or another teacher record these suggestions during this activity.

- For letters of the alphabet that may be more tricky (e.g., Q, V, X, Z), provide students with adjective or word lists such as the one available on Enchanted Learning.com (enchantedlearning.com/wordlist/adjectives.shtml). Descriptive additions to the previous Harlem Renaissance example for these least-used letters of the alphabet might include "Q is for quick-witted writer, Rudolf Fisher"; "V is for the velvety voice of Billy Holiday"; and "Z is for zealous poet Claude McKay."

- Allow students to have many different options in how they illustrate their work. Some may want to use clip art or Google Images, whereas others may choose to create elaborate pen-and-ink drawings. Still others may want to use a fun book-writing tool such as Storybird (www.storybird.com) or Create-Your-Own Comic by Marvel Comics (www.marvel.com).

- Ask an art teacher to coteach part of this lesson with you so that students can be introduced to the different types of art represented in these texts.

- If some students in the classroom are emerging readers or have individual goals related to literacy, you could work with a speech therapist, reading teacher, or other collaborative partner to help the student construct a product that can be used to practice fluency, decoding, and other related skills. This may involve working with the learner and her or his group as they choose the vocabulary for the book and offering strategies as he or she reads certain passages.

- Consider publishing some of the books created in the classroom. Students who enjoy using this type of tool to study might appreciate reading a "real" book created by classmates. Visit sites such as Shutterfly (www.shutterfly.com) and Snapfish (www.snapfish.com) to learn more about the publishing process.

- Write an electronic book as a class. Create a shared Google doc, and assign each student in the class a different letter of the alphabet. Have students add their contributions synchronously during a designated writing time.

IDEAS FOR USING THIS STRUCTURE

_____
_____
_____
_____
_____
_____
_____
_____
_____
_____
_____
_____
_____
_____
_____
_____
_____
_____
_____

AFTER USING THIS STRUCTURE

Did students learn what I intended? Were all students engaged? What changes might be needed to maximize engagement and participation for specific students? How can other team members be involved in co-teaching or instructional support?

_____
_____
_____
_____
_____
_____
_____
_____
_____
_____
_____
_____
_____
_____
_____
_____

Top 10 Lists

Although not every teacher may be as acerbic or clever as David Letterman, who made this format famous on his talk show, anyone can bring the energy and fun of *Top 10 Lists* into the classroom to make review, assessment, and end-of-unit or end-of-year reflection more memorable and more meaningful.

Directions

- Put students into groups of about five or six.

- Give each group a set of materials, including markers, a piece of chart paper, and possibly old magazines or other scrap paper.

- Ask students to consider all they learned during a given day, week, lesson, unit, or year. Then, tell them to narrow their ideas to 10 and create a formal list of these ideas. Give them freedom to create their list in any way they want but ask them to fill their chart paper and to write using dark ink and big letters because these lists will be posted for others to see and use.

- Encourage students to use color and images and to be creative with their language and the text itself (e.g., use block letters for important words, underline key concepts). Remind them that these lists will be used to help others learn, remember, and review.

- Ask students to think of a creative way to present their lists. They might read it off humorously as a television host would, or they could simply display the list and ask classmates to chant the items with them.

- Post the lists around the room for several days (or even weeks) to reinforce reviewed content.

Examples

- A sixth-grade teacher used *Top 10 Lists* to assess student understanding of a unit on fractions. Some of the items on the lists included, "The least common multiple is the smallest number that two or more numbers will divide into evenly" and "A prime number is a whole number that is only divisible by itself and one." Students spent an entire class period creating the lists and making their posters and another class period presenting their creations to one another. The teacher then posted the lists around the room and around the school, putting one on the classroom ceiling, another on the door, and one in each of the student bathrooms. Although the teacher spent only two weeks on the fractions unit, her students remembered the content long after she taught it.

- One high school teacher used this structure as a classroom management tool. She began by asking students to generate ideas on what not to do in the classroom. She invited them to describe a classroom out of control and encouraged them to be creative and "off the wall." What follow are the first entries on the list "Top 10 Ways *Not* to Behave in This Classroom":

  1. Pretending to be listening to the teacher's lecture while texting your cousin Jimmy.

  2. Asking to sharpen your pencil 44 times during one class period.

3. Trying to throw corn chips through another student's hoop earrings.

4. Riding a pig or other domesticated animal into the classroom.

After completing this list, students discussed how they would like their classmates to act and how they might convert these ideas into a few simple rules.

Another Version of This Activity

To extend this activity as a form of celebration, students can generate lists that exemplify positive traits or actions of an individual or group—for example, "The Top 10 Reasons Why Ms. Jones Is an Awesome Teacher" or "The Top 10 Reasons Why Room 506 Deserves a Pizza Party."

Methods to Maximize Engagement and Participation

- Have students jot their own individual ideas down on tablets or index cards and bring them to the group. This ensures that each group has several ideas to draw from as they begin creating their collaborative products.

- Allow artistic or particularly creative students to illustrate or embellish the lists in ways that might help readers of the poster remember the content.

- Select a number of pictures related to the lesson or unit. Allow students who are not yet able to write to select one of these pictures to add to their group's list. Group members can then write a list item related to the picture.

- Provide roles for group members that match their strengths. You might, for instance, have one student read portions of the text aloud, another write specific entries, and still another check for spelling and grammatical errors before the list is finalized.

- To ensure that everyone contributes something, tell students that each member of the group must generate one idea before the group can work collaboratively to finish the list.

IDEAS FOR USING THIS STRUCTURE ✎

_____
_____
_____
_____
_____
_____
_____
_____
_____
_____
_____
_____
_____
_____
_____
_____

AFTER USING THIS STRUCTURE

Did students learn what I intended? Were all students engaged? What changes might be needed to maximize engagement and participation for specific students? How can other team members be involved in co-teaching or instructional support?

_____
_____
_____
_____
_____
_____
_____
_____
_____
_____
_____
_____
_____
_____

Catch!

Catch!, a high-energy activity borrowed from professional trainer Sharon Bowman (2003), can be used to begin an activity, class, or day if you need to jolt students back into material already covered or you can insert it at the end of an activity, class, or day if you want to remind students of all they have just learned.

It is a nice closer or celebration strategy for the diverse classroom, as it gives all students an opportunity to talk, prevents some learners from monopolizing the discussion, and keeps others from avoiding it. Because the pace and sequence of respondents is controlled by the students, there is an element of surprise that holds the attention of those participating.

Directions

- Ask students to stand in a circle and face one another.
- Announce that you are holding a "response object" and that anyone who holds this object will be asked to share something. The object can be anything from a beach ball to a stuffed toy to a rubber eraser. It can be fun to choose something that is related to course content in some way. For instance, during geography lessons, a teacher had students toss a plush globe around the circle. A high school psychology teacher used an inflatable, illustrated brain for the exercise.
- Tell the students that when they catch the object, they need to share something they learned in the day, unit, lesson, or year. Of course, many other prompts or questions would also work well with this structure, including the following:
  - Share a question you still have about the content.
  - What is one thing you still want to learn?
  - What was the hardest/most interesting/most forgettable/most exciting/most annoying/most surprising thing you learned?
- When one person has shared a thought, have him or her select another student (one who has not yet shared) in the circle and toss the object to that person.
- Keep the response object moving around the group until everyone has shared at least one idea.

Implementation Tip

Have students move together in a tight formation so you don't have the object flying across the room, under desks, into furniture or windows, or out of the door. In addition, you might suggest that students make eye contact with a person before throwing it to them or even require that they say the person's name so that individual has time to get ready for the toss.

Examples

- An English teacher regularly used this structure at the end of her classes to have students quickly review the grammar concept she was teaching that day. One day, for instance, she tossed a ball around the classroom and had students name irregular verbs. As students caught the ball, they had to either name an irregular verb or repeat one that a classmate had named.

- A middle school physical education teacher ended all of her units with this structure. It gave her opportunities to review the standards-based content with her students (e.g., rules of games, parts and functions of the body) without breaking from the active and cooperative spirit of her class. When possible, she used objects related to the unit of study, such as a foam football for the unit on that sport.

Methods to Maximize Engagement and Participation

- Allow students to pass if they need more time to generate an idea.

- Have some students (or all) write their ideas down on an index card or sticky note and bring it into the circle in case they forget their idea when the object comes their way.

- Split the class and play *Catch!* with two smaller groups to save time and to give all learners more time to share.

- Give students the option of offering a unique idea or repeating a response that has already been shared.

- Limit responses to one-word phrases to make the game more lively.

IDEAS FOR USING THIS STRUCTURE ✎

AFTER USING THIS STRUCTURE

Did students learn what I intended? Were all students engaged? What changes might be needed to maximize engagement and participation for specific students? How can other team members be involved in co-teaching or instructional support?

Sixty-Second Commercial

Light the lights. Cue the cameras. It's time to shoot a commercial.

This entertaining activity is borrowed from corporate trainers (Solem & Pike, 1998) and works as a memorable review of course material. It can also serve as a celebration of a learning experience, a unit, or even a school year. *Sixty-Second Commercial* exploits student knowledge of both television and popular culture and gives dramatic and outgoing students, in particular, opportunities to shine.

Directions

- Put students into small groups and ask them to create a 60-second television commercial that features a class topic. The commercial should, as much as possible, emphasize elements of curriculum, and the ad should contain a slogan to help the group and all others in the class better remember the content (e.g., "Teapot Dome—It's a Scandal, Not a Household Item!").

- Encourage students to act out the commercial using techniques they see on television (e.g., have an expert or celebrity sell the topic, show a happy family, use statistics).

- Give ample time for brainstorming ideas and provide a box of props that might be used by the groups in their mini-productions.

- Give each team one minute to present its ad to the class.

- After the presentations, ask students to share what they learned from the ads.

Implementation Tip

Be sure to give students enough time to generate ideas and rehearse. The brainstorming alone may take 20 minutes or more. Although it may be tempting to cut the process short to save time, teachers often find that this activity is one of the things that students remember most about the unit or the class. When students are brainstorming, they are, in essence, thinking about ways to make the information memorable and catchy. In other words, they are doing what good teachers do! Therefore, the time is usually well spent, and although it may be useful to monitor the groups carefully to be sure they are working efficiently, be careful not to cut the creative process too short.

Example

- A ninth-grade English teacher had students perform commercials on the parts of speech to prepare them for a final exam. She gave each group a worksheet with information she wanted them to incorporate into their commercials (ensuring that the most critical concepts would be reviewed) and reminded all the groups that the ultimate goal was to create an advertisement that would help fellow students recall the information on the upcoming exam. She then reviewed some of the strategies that advertisers use to help people remember their products (e.g., jingles, alliteration, shock, humor).

The commercials were successful in that students learned the content while they prepared the ads and reported that they were easily able to recall slogans from the ads (e.g., "Need to Verb a Noun? Lucky You! Gerund Is in Town!") when they were taking their tests.

Methods to Maximize Engagement and Participation

- Video record the commercials; put them on a class wiki for students to watch repeatedly if they need a review.

- To help students who are Deaf or hard of hearing or those who may need a multimodal approach to instruction, ask groups to use close captioning in their commercials. While the commercial "plays," a student can flip cue cards on the side of the actors, give all learners a copy of the script so everyone can follow along, or share the lines one by one on the interactive whiteboard.

- Consider assigning one or two students the role of director. This person's job is to make sure that the commercials all have different messages and that students will learn something new from each presentation.

- To make sure students are learning the content, you might have groups perform the commercials repeatedly over the course of a week or month. These reruns give everyone (the groups themselves and the audience) several opportunities to learn the content, as well as provide an enjoyable way to punctuate a lesson or wake up a tired group. Another benefit of the repeated viewings is that they make the material so memorable; before a test (or even during), the teacher or the students can hum or sing part of a jingle to aid in the recall of concepts.

IDEAS FOR USING THIS STRUCTURE ✐

AFTER USING THIS STRUCTURE

Did students learn what I intended? Were all students engaged? What changes might be needed to maximize engagement and participation for specific students? How can other team members be involved in co-teaching or instructional support?

Collaborative Quiz

The typical anxiety associated with testing evaporates (or at least is diminished) when students have opportunities not only to construct the test itself but to work with others to generate the answers. With *Collaborative Quiz,* a low-stress cooperative learning technique, students can show what they know and prepare for other, more formal assessments without boredom, tension, or tedium.

Directions

- Take 10 to 15 minutes for students to review a chapter from their book or a set of concepts from a unit.

- Ask each of them to develop one or two quiz questions from this material. Inform them that these questions may show up on an assessment that will be given to the whole class.

- Then, informally, ask students to share their questions and provide the related answers (this part of the process serves as a review for the upcoming quiz). At the end of that exercise, collect the questions.

- The following day (or at another time in the future), distribute a quiz that has been assembled entirely from the questions submitted by the students. The familiarity of the material will decrease the usual test day rumblings, as will the next direction.

- Inform students that they not only created the quiz collaboratively but that they will also take the quiz collaboratively.

- Break them into pairs or small groups.

- Distribute one quiz to each student. Ask them to assign the role of scribe to someone in their group. Inform them that only one of the quizzes can be submitted, so the scribe will be working on the only quiz that the teacher will see.

Implementation Tip

Although it is possible to engage in this structure in one classroom (with students using low voices), it may be easier to manage if groups are able to spread out in separate spaces for the quiz itself. Potential areas for quiz administration include the library, the hallway, and the main office.

Example

- A fourth-grade teacher used *Collaborative Quiz* to prepare her students for upcoming standardized tests. Because the mere mention of these tests makes some students feel nervous, lethargic, or both, she used this technique to make test time more social and, therefore, more enjoyable. The teacher was not surprised to learn that the technique also seemed to better prepare students for the test. Having students generate quiz questions seemed to grab their interest.

Giving them time to talk, both about content and the testing situation itself, appeared to promote deeper learning. She was especially impressed with the comments she heard from students as they discussed the final question on the test (the one question she had generated herself): "Share one strategy you use to succeed on tests." By using this technique, learners were able not only to prepare for the content they would see on the future test, but also to learn concrete study strategies. This sharing helped them all and in particular aided students who didn't traditionally do well in testing situations.

Methods to Maximize Engagement and Participation

- To generate more interest, allow students to submit test questions written as answers (in the style of the television game show *Jeopardy!*). Some students will be motivated by the novelty of such a task and may even come up with more complex material due to the unique challenge.

- Before generating questions on their own, some students will need to see sample questions related to the material being studied and examples of different types of quiz questions (e.g., matching, true/false, multiple choice, fill in the blank). For students who need even more support to generate ideas, a sample quiz with several questions could be provided, and these learners could be asked to highlight the one or two questions they would like to see on the quiz. The sample questions could be coded as easy, medium, or high difficulty.

- On quiz day, be sure that the students assigned to be the scribes will be able to handle the tasks of writing on demand and organizing thoughts and ideas quickly. If this will be challenging for many of the students, consider assigning the role to multiple students, with each taking a short turn. You might also assign other roles, such as timekeeper, proofreader, collaboration monitor, and encourager.

- Add a few of your own questions to the test, focusing on items related to group-functioning and test-taking behaviors (e.g., "What is one strategy you can use to remain alert and focused during the test-taking process?" and "What is one study or flashcard app you can use to prepare for a test?").

IDEAS FOR USING THIS STRUCTURE ✎

_____
_____
_____
_____
_____
_____
_____
_____
_____
_____
_____
_____
_____
_____
_____
_____
_____
_____
_____
_____

AFTER USING THIS STRUCTURE

Did students learn what I intended? Were all students engaged? What changes might be needed to maximize engagement and participation for specific students? How can other team members be involved in co-teaching or instructional support?

_____
_____
_____
_____
_____
_____
_____
_____
_____
_____
_____
_____
_____
_____
_____

Human Treasure Hunt

Camp counselors, scout leaders, and church group organizers alike have used this activity to break the ice at a meeting or inspire laughter at a social gathering. *Human Treasure Hunt* can include simple to complex tasks and can include both personal questions (e.g., Find someone who wears socks to bed) and questions related to classroom content (e.g., Find someone who knows the names of the two US senators from Wyoming). This structure lends itself to assessing and celebrating because it affirms the expertise of the members of the classroom before or after learning new material has taken place.

Directions

- Give each student a worksheet containing a series of questions or prompts related to course content. The objective is for students to find an answer to every prompt on their sheet by collecting expertise and information from fellow class members.

- Announce the rules for the game:
  - Get only one answer from each student you approach.
  - If you get an answer from a student, you need to give an answer to her or him.

- Tell students to walk around the room, start conversations with peers, ask questions, and secure answers to the hunt questions.

- When everyone finishes their hunts, direct them to come back to their seats. Review answers as a group, correct any errors in responses, and discuss how and what students learned from their peers.

Implementation Tip

To get students moving immediately, tell them they are not allowed to work with anyone in their row (or table) for the first two or three items of the treasure hunt. You may even want to assign partners for the first few items of the hunt.

Example

- A high school science teacher asked students to complete a Human Treasure Hunt as an end-of-quarter review (see Figure 5.3). All students were asked to contribute potential questions for the hunt, and the teacher constructed the worksheet entirely from student-generated items. As students circulated around the room gathering information from one another, the teacher listened in on conversations to assess readiness for the exam and to provide individual students with on-the-spot instruction on key points. One student with exceptional ability in science already knew most of the concepts on the sheet before beginning the exercise, so the teacher allowed him to replace three questions with three new "challenge prompts" that he pulled from outside reading and from a quick Internet search. This student was then allowed to approach individuals with these enrichment questions as part of the treasure hunt activity.

Figure 5.3 *Human Treasure Hunt:* **Physical Science Example**

Human Treasure Hunt

Clipart.com.

Name _____

The goal of this activity is to learn as much as you can from the experts in this classroom. You may get only one answer from each person you approach, and that person may get only one answer from you.

1. Find a person who can draw a picture of "a force acting through a distance" (work).

```



```

Have this artist sign here: _____

2. Find someone who can name a use of radioactivity.

_____

Have this science expert sign here: _____

3. Find someone who can explain a type of pulley you use in everyday life.

_____

_____

Have this observant classmate sign here: _____

4. Find someone who will act out, explain, or draw the Doppler effect.

```



```

Have this creative individual sign here: _____

After you are finished, walk around the room and help your classmates finish their treasure hunts.

Methods to Maximize Engagement and Participation

- Have a few students serve as "hunt helpers." Their job is to walk around and offer assistance to students who are having difficulty completing their forms. Helpers can provide information or, preferably, point students to others who have expertise in certain areas and who may have helped other students with the same item on the hunt form.

- Let students generate a few of their own items as they wander around the room or before the hunt begins.

- If a peer cannot answer a question verbally, her or his classmate can invent a question that can be answered by gesturing, drawing, or pointing to items in the classroom or in the textbook. A question such as "Find someone who can sign the elements that make up water (H_2O)" pushes every student to learn alternative ways of expressing their knowledge.

- Students who have specific skills, who have mastered selected content, or who have a limited repertoire of facts can rehearse unique information on which they are experts in advance of this activity. Prompts can be written on other students' treasure hunt forms to alert them to their classmates' expertise—for example, "Remember to ask Jim about the symbols for iron and helium," or "Dagne and Russ both know about Sacagawea's role on the Lewis and Clark expedition."

- Some students may be given fewer items to find on their scavenger hunt forms if communication or movement issues affect their speed in acquiring information. In fact, you may want to distribute a few different versions of the hunt form if this issue arises. This way, students can use the form that is more appropriate for their needs, reading level, or learning goals, and participants will have a wider variety of questions to answer if different forms contain different items.

- Allow students needing more challenge to create the entire hunt form for the group.

- Allow students to peek at their textbook, class notes, or certain websites if they need assistance to answer a question.

- This activity gives teachers an opportunity to highlight the expertise, experiences, specific gifts, or strengths of individual learners. If a student has just moved from Saudi Arabia, the teacher might include an item related to the geography of the Middle East. If a book-loving student has a particular interest in *Alice in Wonderland,* the treasure hunt might include an item asking students to act out or draw a scene from the popular book.

IDEAS FOR USING THIS STRUCTURE

AFTER USING THIS STRUCTURE

Did students learn what I intended? Were all students engaged? What changes might be needed to maximize engagement and participation for specific students? How can other team members be involved in co-teaching or instructional support?

Act Like It!

Act Like It! is a classroom game that, although silly, often helps learners retain information they otherwise might not. In this activity, students work in small teams to "become" words, concepts, ideas, or things. Teachers can either assign all groups the same word or concept or give different groups different (but related) words or concepts. Depending on the students' needs, the teacher may choose to offer options that are very concrete, such as *pyramid* or *microscope,* or ones that are more abstract and complex, such as *community, element, cosine,* or *imagery.*

Directions

- Examine your lesson. Identify the words, ideas, or concepts students need to study, understand, and discuss.

- Put students into small groups.

- Assign one or more of these words, ideas, or concepts to each group of students, or give every group the same word, idea, or concept.

- Tell students they are responsible for acting out or dramatically representing the word, idea, or concept assigned. For instance, a group might get this assignment: "You are the desert ecosystem. Act like it!"

- Give groups a short period of time to generate ideas for the performances. You can allow props or makeshift costumes if time permits.

- The assigned referents might be known to everyone in the room, or the class might be charged with guessing the word, idea, or concept as the group performs.

- Add criteria to make the performances a little more formal and, potentially, more structured and useful. For instance, you might require that the performances last at least a minute, use at least two props, include a visual support, and repeat an important term or word at least twice.

Examples

- In a ninth-grade science lesson, a teacher asked his students, in groups of four, to act out the concepts of *fusion* and *fission.* Although all of the learners essentially engaged in the same types of behaviors when they performed (rushing together into a clump and then fleeing to all corners of the classroom), each group had its own interpretation, and each mini-presentation helped the students remember the movement of atoms in each of the examples come exam time.

- In a language arts lesson, the teacher asked students to act like the following vocabulary words: *evocative, nefarious, pithy, onerous, precocious, sordid,* and *restitution.* Each group had to act out each one of the words while the audience guessed which skit represented which word from the list. This exercise was especially useful for Renee, a student on the autism spectrum. Renee found the visual imagery helpful to learn new words (especially those with abstract meanings). The lighthearted atmosphere of the activity helped her feel relaxed, which was in contrast to the feeling of stress she often experienced during other language-focused lessons.

Methods to Maximize Engagement and Participation

- Provide a box of costumes and props for students to use in their acts, or give them items such as scrap paper, blankets, paper towels, ribbons, paper plates, and school supplies in order to create props on the spot.

- For students who need more challenge, assign charades that are more abstract, or allow these learners to write their own *Act Like It!* prompts.

- Ask students to engage in impromptu revisions of each skit. Assign specific roles for this purpose. For instance, one student might be asked to fact check and another might suggest helpful visuals. Still another might work on sound (e.g., write dialogue, suggest certain types of music) to add meaning to the performance.

IDEAS FOR USING THIS STRUCTURE

_____
_____
_____
_____
_____
_____
_____
_____
_____
_____
_____
_____
_____
_____
_____
_____

AFTER USING THIS STRUCTURE

Did students learn what I intended? Were all students engaged? What changes might be needed to maximize engagement and participation for specific students? How can other team members be involved in co-teaching or instructional support?

_____
_____
_____
_____
_____
_____
_____
_____
_____
_____
_____
_____
_____
_____
_____
_____
_____

A Final Note

In the interim between the first edition of this book and the completion of the second edition, Alice was asked to contribute an entry defining *joyful learning* to the *Encyclopedia of the Sciences of Learning,* the first encyclopedia covering all sectors, paradigms, and movements of the sciences of learning from their origins through the present. We were thrilled at this opportunity because it indicated international recognition that the concept of joyful learning is indeed a viable theoretical idea. Here is the formal definition rendered for the encyclopedia:

> *Joy* can be defined as an emotion evoked by well-being. To be *joyful* means experiencing delight or happiness caused by something pleasing or gratifying. Consequently, the term *joyful learning* (Udvari-Solner & Kluth, 2007) in the context of education refers to the positive intellectual and emotional state of the learner(s). This state or experience is achieved when an individual or group is deriving pleasure and a sense of satisfaction from the process of learning. Characteristics of joyful learning include being highly engaged in the task or experience while having a sense of wonder and curiosity. Typically, educators and their students both benefit from and feel synchronicity in the teaching/learning experience. There is a sense of shared interest and purpose. Learners of all abilities interact meaningfully with the educational content while also interacting with one another in supportive academic and social interchanges that encourage risk-taking. The individual is an active rather than passive agent in his/her learning. The atmosphere or climate of the learning environment is not typically one of quiet, routine, or rote activities but one of discovery, novelty, excitement, and positivity. Joyful learning may occur spontaneously in classrooms but can be engineered through the use of specific *active and collaborative instructional strategies* (Udvari-Solner, 2012c, p. 1665).

Since the inception of this book, we have been on a quest to find other concepts, theories, and practices that align with what we conceptualize as joyful learning. We have found two very notable connections. Joyful learning seems most closely related to the theoretical work of Mihály Csíkszentmihály and his concept of *flow* (Csíkszentmihály, 1990). Csíkszentmihály researched "positive psychology" and investigated human strengths in thinking and behaviors such as intrinsic motivation, creativity, and optimism. In the seminal book *Flow: The Psychology of Optimal Experience* (1990), he proposed there is a mental state of operation in which the person is completely involved in an activity for its own sake and is fully immersed and feels energized by the process of engagement. Emotions are not only channeled toward and aligned with the activity, but the individual can receive great joy from performing the task. Joyful learning also promotes this sense of energized focus and full involvement that results in an innately positive experience. In essence, learning takes place for the sake of learning. Joyful learning and the notion of flow hold in common several elements that mark the experience:

- There are clear goals for the learner in which expectations are attainable yet challenging.

- There is a high level of concentration and focus on the task of interest.

- The individual is not self-conscious and limited by anxiety or doubt in his or her abilities to learn.

- There is personal control or agency in the learning event.

- The experience is intrinsically rewarding and thereby promotes longer periods of engagement that may not be consciously perceived by the learner (i.e., the adage "Time flies" is realized).

- Mechanisms for specific and immediate feedback are available to the learner to assess success.

Flow is most often referenced as single-minded immersion; however, an expressed goal in joyful learning is to create opportunities for *synchronous engagement* and maximal involvement of a wide range of learners.

A second "big idea" connected to joyful learning is mindful learning, a notion advanced by Harvard psychology professor Ellen Langer (1997). Two standard approaches to learning are top-down and bottom-up. One top-down approach is lecturing to students, whereby the teacher possesses the "relevant" information and imparts it to the students to be memorized and applied. Characteristic of a bottom-up approach is the idea that learning must involve breaking down a task into discrete parts and engaging in repeated practice by prescribed methods until basic skills are adequately acquired. Langer suggests these two traditional approaches may lead to thoughtless or mechanical interaction with the skill or concept, thereby hindering discovery and deeper understanding. In contrast, learning in a mindful state is facilitated by (1) openness to novelty, (2) alertness to distinction or awareness of discriminatory details, (3) sensitivity to different contexts, (4) awareness of multiple perspectives, and (5) orientation in the present. Like the concept of mindfulness, joyful learning challenges habitual or traditional teaching paradigms and emphasizes the creation of positive and even enjoyable learning processes.

Classrooms and schools worldwide have been criticized for learning climates that instill anxiety and boredom and impede students' innate interest and spirit to learn (Willis, 2007b; Wolk, 2008). Too often, the implicit messages sent to students are that schooling is simply work and drudgery; that if you are having a sense of enjoyment or fun, learning won't be effective; and that joy should be earned or even reserved for environments other than school. To counter these deleterious messages, "joy-focused" educators have proposed guiding principles to help teachers design learning experiences that are appropriately inviting, motivating, and stimulating (Willis, 2007a, 2007b; Wolk, 2008). These principles include the following:

- Make learning relevant by connecting content whenever possible to what is personally interesting, motivating, and emotionally important to students. Both the students and the teacher should be able to articulate *what* is being learned as well as *why* it has relevance and importance in the learners' present and future lives.

- Sanction time for intellectual and emotional breaks so that the brain can recoup and be ready for learning throughout the day.

- Be aware of when learning activities are needlessly stressful and therefore create negative associations with the situation, content, and people. When students are learning new or more challenging information, create opportunities to explore the concepts without high-stakes consequences.

- Encourage independent discovery by allowing time for students to find what intrigues them. Time for independent or guided exploration is the foundation for fostering internal motivation.

- Provide choice. Consider how students can have agency in what they learn and how they learn it. Wolk (2008) suggests designating time for students to collaborate with teachers to create inquiry-based investigations from student-initiated ideas. We encourage educators to teach students a range of active and collaborative learning strategies and then empower them to select the approach that would best facilitate their learning.

- Create learning spaces that facilitate collaboration and shared inquiry. Use options other than traditional classroom configurations of desks in rows, and establish places where both large and small groups of students can move, sit, and interact with each other and with learning materials.

Of course, you can also inspire joy by using the strategies in this book! In sum, we hope we have created a text that you, the reader, will find useful. More than that, however, we hope that we have created a tool that might help many of you create classrooms that are inviting and accessible for a larger variety of learners. Although we do want this text to serve as a quick, desktop, lesson-planning reference, we are also hoping that it can inspire changes in classroom practice and in the number of students who receive access to meaningful curriculum and instruction in general education classrooms.

If you find this text useful and particularly if it helps you support students with unique learning profiles, reach students who have not traditionally had success in the classroom, or create more inclusive opportunities for students with disabilities, please write and let us know (Alice Udvari-Solner, alice@education.wisc.edu, and Paula Kluth, paula.kluth@gmail.com). We are interested in learning more about the potential of active instruction as a response to—if not a remedy for—everything from challenging behavior to boredom to academic struggles. Good luck—we wish you success, and we hope to hear from you!

References

American Association for the Advancement of Science. (1989). *Science for all Americans: Project 2061.* New York, NY: Oxford University Press.

Bandura, A. (1977*). Social learning theory.* New York, NY: General Learning Press.

Beichner, R. (2014). History and evolution of active learning spaces [Special issue]. *New Directions for Teaching and Learning, 137,* 9–16.

Bennett, B., Rolheiser, C., & Stevahn, L. (1991). *Cooperative learning: Where heart meets mind.* Toronto, Canada: Educational Connections.

Black, D. S., & Fernando, R. (2013). Mindfulness training and classroom behavior among lower-income and ethnic minority elementary school children. *Journal of Child and Family Studies, 22,* 1–5.

Bonwell, C., & Eisen, J. (1991, September). *Active learning: Creating excitement in the classroom* (ED340272). Washington, DC: George Washington University.

Bowman, S. (2003). *How to give it so they get it.* Glenbrook, NV: Bowperson.

Boyle, J. (2001). Enhancing the note-taking skills of students with mild disabilities. *Intervention in School and Clinic, 36,* 221–224.

Boyles, N. (2012, December/2013, January). Closing in on close reading. *Educational Leadership, 70*(4), 36–41.

Buehl, D. (1995). *Classroom strategies for interactive learning.* Schofield: Wisconsin State Reading Association.

Calkins, L., & Oxenhorn, A. (2003). *Small moments: Personal narrative writing.* Portsmouth, NH: Heinemann.

Causton, J., Udvari-Solner, A., & Richmond, K. (2016). Creating educational adaptations, accommodations and modifications. In F. Orelove, D. Sobsey, & D. Gilles (Eds.), *Educating students with severe and multiple disabilities: A collaborative approach* (5th ed., pp. 407–435). Baltimore, MD: Brookes.

Chickering, A., & Gamson, Z. F. (1987). Seven principles for good practice. *American Association for Higher Education Bulletin, 39,* 3–7.

Cole, R. (2001). *More strategies for educating everybody's children.* Alexandria, VA: Association for Supervision and Curriculum Development.

Core-Plus Mathematics Project. (2005). *CPMP course 1 units.* Retrieved June 20, 2007, from http://www.wmich.edu/cpmp/

Csíkszentmihály, M. (1990). *Flow: The psychology of optimal experience.* New York, NY: Harper and Row.

Davidson, E., & Schniedewind, N. (1998). *Open minds to equality: A sourcebook of learning activities to affirm diversity and promote equity* (2nd ed.). Needham Heights, MA: Allyn & Bacon.

Draper, R. (1997). Active learning in mathematics: Desktop teaching. *Mathematics Teacher, 90,* 622–625.

Falvey, M., Givner, C., Villa, R., & Thousand, J. (2017). An inclusive school: Providing access and success for all. In R. Villa & J. Thousand (Eds.), *Leading an inclusive school* (pp. 7–16). Alexandria, VA: Association for Supervision and Curriculum Development.

Falvey, M. A., & Givner, C. C. (2005). What is an inclusive school? In R. Villa & J. Thousand (Eds.), *Creating an inclusive school* (pp. 1–26). Alexandria VA: Association for Supervision and Curriculum Development.

Fisher, D., & Roach, V. (1999). *Opening doors: Connecting students to curriculum, classmates, and learning.* Colorado Springs, CO: PEAK Parent Center.

Fisher, D., Sax, C., & Pumpian, I. (1999). *Inclusive high schools: Learning from contemporary classrooms.* Baltimore, MD: Brookes.

Flook, L., Goldberg, S. B., Pinger, L., & Davidson, R. J. (2015). Promoting prosocial behavior and self-regulatory skills in preschool children through a mindfulness-based kindness curriculum. *Developmental Psychology, 51*(1), 44–51.

Freeman, S., Eddy, S., McDonough, M., Smith, M., Okoroafor, N., Jordt, H., & Wenderoth, M. P. (2014). Active learning increases student performance in science, engineering, and mathematics. *Proceedings of the National Academy of Sciences USA, 111*(23), 8410–8415.

Freire, P. (1970). *Pedagogy of the oppressed.* New York, NY: Continuum.

Gadotti, M. (1994). *Reading Paulo Freire: His life & work.* Albany: State University of New York Press.

Gibbs, J. (1995). *Tribes: A new way of learning and being together.* Sausalito, CA: Center Source Systems.

González, N., Moll, L., & Amanti, C. (2005). *Funds of knowledge: Theorizing practices in households, communities, and classrooms.* Mahwah, NJ: Erlbaum.

Goodwin, B. (2015). Research says promising, but incomplete results for mindfulness. *Educational Leadership, 73*(2), 78–79.

Harmin, M. (1994). *Inspiring active learning: A handbook for teachers.* Alexandria, VA: Association for Supervision and Curriculum Development.

Harmin, M., & Toth, M. (2006). *Inspiring active learning: A complete handbook for teachers* (2nd ed.). Alexandria, VA: Association for Supervision and Curriculum Development.

Harry, B., & Klingner, J. (2005). *Why are so many minority students in special education? Understanding race & disability in schools.* New York, NY: Teachers College Press.

Hartley, J., & Davies, I. K. (1978). Note taking: A critical review. *Programmed Learning and Educational Technology, 15,* 207–224.

Hohmann, M., Epstein, A., & Wiekart, A. (2008). *Educating young children: Active learning practices for preschool and child care programs* (3rd ed.). Ypsilanti, MI: High/Scope Educational Research Foundation.

Howard, P. (1994). *Owner's manual for the brain.* Austin, TX: Leorinian Press.

Jensen, E. (2005). *Teaching with the brain in mind* (2nd ed.). Alexandria, VA: Association for Supervision and Curriculum Development.

Jensen, E. (2009). *Teaching with poverty in mind.* Alexandria, VA: Association for Supervision and Curriculum Development.

Johnson, D., & Johnson, R. (2005). New developments in social independence theory. *Genetic, Social, and General Psychology Monographs, 131*(4), 285–358.

Johnson, D. W., Johnson, R. T., & Smith, K. A. (1998). *Active learning: Cooperation in the college classroom* (2nd ed.). Edina, MN: Interaction Book.

Jorgensen, C. (1998). *Restructuring high schools for all students: Taking inclusion to the next level.* Baltimore, MD: Brookes.

Kagan, S. (1992). *Cooperative learning.* San Clemente, CA: Kagan.

Kahn, P., & Hasbach, P. (Eds.). (2013). *The rediscovery of the wild.* Cambridge, MA: MIT Press.

Kahn, P. H., Jr. (2011). Can technology replace nature? We need actual nature for our physiological and psychological well-being. Retrieved from https://www.psychologytoday.com/blog/human-nature/201106/can-technology-replace-nature

Kasa-Hendrickson, C., & Kluth, P. (2005). "We have to start with inclusion and work it out as we go": Purposeful inclusion for non-verbal students with autism. *International Journal of Whole Schooling, 2*(1), 2–14.

Keyser, M. (2000). Active learning and cooperative learning: Understanding the difference and using both styles effectively. *Research Strategies, 17*(1), 35–44.

Klatt, M., Harpster, K., Browne, E., White, S., & Case-Smith, J. (2013). Feasibility and preliminary outcomes for Move-into-Learning: An arts-based mindfulness classroom intervention. *Journal of Positive Psychology, 8*(3), 233–241.

Kluth, P. (2003). *"You're going to love this kid": Teaching students with autism in the inclusive classroom.* Baltimore, MD: Brookes.

Kluth, P., Straut, D., & Biklen, D. (Eds.). (2003). *Access to academics for all students: Critical approaches to inclusive curriculum, instruction, and policy.* Mahwah, NJ: Erlbaum.

Kuyken, W., Weare, K., Ukoumunne, O. C., Vicary, R., Motton, N., Burnett, R., Cullen, C., Hennelly, S., & Hupert, F. (2013). Effectiveness of the mindfulness in schools programme: Non-randomised controlled feasibility study. *British Journal of Psychiatry, 203*(2), 126–131.

Langer, E. (1997). *The power of mindful learning.* Cambridge, MA: Perseus Books.

Loomans, D., & Kolberg, K. (1993). *The laughing classroom: Everyone's guide to teaching with humor and play.* Tiburon, CA: H. J. Kramer.

Margulies, N., & Maal, N. (2001). *Mapping inner space: Learning and teaching visual mapping.* Chicago: Zephyr Press.

Marzano, R. (2003).*What works in schools: Translating research into action.* Alexandria, VA: Association for Supervision and Curriculum Development.

McIntosh, P. (1990). White privilege: Unpacking the invisible knapsack. *Independent School, 49*(2), 31–35.

Oyler, C. (2001). Democratic classrooms and accessible instruction. *Democracy & Education, 14,* 28–31.

Palinscar, A. S. (1998). Social constructivist perspectives on teaching and learning. *Annual Review of Psychology, 49,* 345–375.

Panitz, T. (1997). Collaborative versus cooperative learning: Comparing the two definitions helps understand the nature of interactive learning. *Cooperative Learning and College Teaching, 8*(2), 68–72.

Parker, J. (1990). *Workshops for active learning.* Vancouver, Canada: JFP Productions.

Paulson, P., & Faust, J. (2010). *Active learning for the college classroom.* Retrieved from http://web.calstatela.edu/dept/chem/chem2/Active/index.htm

Prensky, M. (2001). Digital natives, digital immigrants. *On the Horizon, 9*(5), 1–6.

Prensky, M. R. (2010). *Teaching digital natives: Partnering for real learning.* Newbury Park, CA: Corwin.

Prince, M. (2004, July). Does active learning work? A review of the research. *Journal of Engineering 93*(3), 223–231.

Ratey, J. (2008). *Spark: The revolutionary new science of exercise and the brain.* New York, NY: Little, Brown.

Ratey, J., & Loehr, J. (2011). The positive impact of physical activity on cognition during adulthood: A review of underlying mechanisms, evidence, and recommendations. *Neuroscience Review, 22*(2), 171–185.

Roehl, A., Linga Reddy, S., & Shannon, G. (2013). The flipped classroom: An opportunity to engage millennial students through active learning strategies. *Journal of Family and Consumer Science, 105*(2), 44–49.

Roschelle, J., & Teasley, S. D. (1995). The construction of shared knowledge in collaborative problem solving. In C. O'Malley (Ed.), *Computer supported collaborative learning* (pp. 69–97). New York, NY: Springer.

Rose, D. H., & Meyer, A. (2002). *Teaching every student in the digital age: Universal Design for Learning*. Alexandria, VA: Association for Supervision and Curriculum Development.

Rossi, E. L., & Nimmons, D. (1991). *The 20-minute break: Using the new science of ultradian rhythms*. Los Angeles, CA: Tarcher.

Ruhl, K., Hughes, C., & Schloss, P. (1987). Using the pause procedure to enhance lecture recall. *Teacher Education and Special Education, 10,* 14–18.

Russell, I. J., Hendricson, W. D., & Herbert, R. J. (1984). Effects of lecture information density on medical student achievement. *Journal of Medical Education, 59,* 881–889.

Sapon-Shevin, M. (2007). *Widening the circle: The power of inclusive classrooms*. Boston, MA: Beacon Press.

Sapon-Shevin, M. (2010). *Because we can change the world: A practical guide to building cooperative, inclusive classroom communities* (2nd ed.). Thousand Oaks, CA: Corwin.

Short, K. G., Harste, J., & Burke, C. (1996). *Creating classrooms for authors and inquirers* (2nd ed.). Portsmouth, NH: Heinemann.

Silberman, M. (1996). *Active learning: 101 strategies to teach any subject*. Boston: Allyn & Bacon.

Solem, L., & Pike, B. (1998). *50 creative training closers: Innovative ways to end your training with IMPACT*. San Francisco, CA: Jossey-Bass.

Springer, L., Stanne M. E., & Donovan, S. (1999). Measuring the success of small-group learning in college level SMET teaching: A meta-analysis. *Review of Educational Research, 69,* 21–51.

Thousand, J., Udvari-Solner, A., & Villa, R. (2017). Differentiated instruction: Access to general education curriculum for all. In R. Villa & J. Thousand (Eds.), *Leading an inclusive school* (pp. 117–143). Alexandria, VA: Association for Supervision and Curriculum Development.

Tomlinson, C. (1995). *How to differentiate instruction in mixed-ability classrooms*. Alexandria, VA: Association for Supervision and Curriculum Development.

Tomlinson, C. (2003). *Fulfilling the promise of the differentiated classroom: Strategies and tools for responsive teaching*. Alexandria, VA: Association for Supervision and Curriculum Development.

Udvari-Solner, A. (1993). *Curricular adaptations: Accommodating the instructional needs of diverse learners in the context of general education classrooms* (Rev. ed.). Topeka: Kansas State Department of Education.

Udvari-Solner, A. (1995). A process for adapting curriculum in inclusive classrooms. In R. Villa & J. Thousand (Eds.), *Creating an inclusive school* (pp. 110–124). Alexandria, VA: Association for Supervision and Curriculum Development.

Udvari-Solner, A. (1996a). Examining teacher thinking: Constructing a process to design curricular adaptations. *Remedial and Special Education, 17,* 245–254.

Udvari-Solner, A. (1996b). Theoretical influences on the establishment of inclusive practices. *Cambridge Journal of Education, 26*(1), 101–119.

Udvari-Solner, A. (1997). Inclusive education. In C. Grant & G. Ladson-Billings (Eds.), *The dictionary of multi-cultural education* (pp. 141–144). Phoenix, AZ: Oryx Press.

Udvari-Solner, A. (2003). Leading social change in collaborative and inclusive practice: The journey of a middle school. *Impact: Feature Issue on Revisiting Inclusive K–12 Education, 16*(1). Retrieved June 20, 2007, from http://ici.umn.edu/products/ impact/161/prof3.html

Udvari-Solner, A. (2012a). Collaborative learning. In N. M. Seel (Ed.), *Encyclopedia of the sciences of learning* (pp. 631–634). New York, NY: Springer.

Udvari-Solner, A. (2012b). Collaborative learning strategies. In N. M. Seel (Ed.), *Encyclopedia of the sciences of learning* (pp. 636–639). New York, NY: Springer.

Udvari-Solner, A. (2012c). Joyful learning. In N. M. Seel (Ed.), *Encyclopedia of the sciences of learning* (pp. 1665–1667). New York, NY: Springer.

Udvari-Solner, A., Ahlgren-Bouchard, K., & Harell, K. (2016). Instructing students with severe and multiple disabilities in inclusive classrooms. In F. Orelove, D. Sobsey., & D. Gilles (Eds.), *Educating students with severe and multiple disabilities: A collaborative approach* (5th ed., pp. 351–405). Baltimore, MD: Brookes.

Udvari-Solner, A., & Keyes, M. (2000). "We're on the train and we've left the station, but we haven't gotten to the next stop": Chronicles of administrative leadership toward inclusive reform. In R. Villa & J. Thousand (Eds.), *Restructuring for a caring and effective education: Piecing the puzzle together* (2nd ed.). Baltimore, MD: Brookes.

Udvari-Solner, A., & Kluth, P. (2007). *Joyful learning: Active and collaborative learning in inclusive classrooms.* Thousand Oaks, CA: Corwin.

Udvari-Solner, A., & Thousand, J. (1996). Creating a responsive curriculum for inclusive schools. *Remedial and Special Education, 17,* 182–192.

Udvari-Solner, A., Villa, R., & Thousand, J. (2002). Access to the general education curriculum for all: The universal design process. In J. Thousand, R. Villa, & A. Nevin (Eds.), *Creativity and collaboration: A practical guide to empowering students and teachers* (pp. 85–103). Baltimore, MD: Brookes.

Udvari-Solner, A., Villa, R., & Thousand, J. (2005). Access to the general education curriculum for all: The universal design process. In R. Villa & J. Thousand (Eds.), *Creating an inclusive school* (2nd ed., pp. 134–155). Alexandria, VA: Association for Supervision and Curriculum Development.

Villa, R., & Thousand, J. (Eds.). (2005). *Creating an inclusive school* (2nd ed.). Alexandria, VA: Association for Supervision and Curriculum Development.

Villa, R., & Thousand, J. (Eds.). (2017). *Leading an inclusive school.* Alexandra, VA: Association for Supervision and Curriculum Development.

Vygotsky, L. S. (1978). *Mind in society.* Cambridge, MA: Harvard University Press.

Willis, J. (2007a). *Brain-friendly strategies for the inclusion classroom.* Alexandria, VA: Association for Supervision and Curriculum Development.

Willis, J. (2007b). The neuroscience of joyful education. *Educational Leadership, 64*(9).

Wilson, M., & Gerber, L. E. (2008). How generational theory can improve teaching: Strategies for working with the "millennials." *Currents in Teaching and Learning, 1*(1), 29–44.

Wolk, S. (2008). Joy in school. *Educational Leadership, 66*(1), 8–15.

Index

A SAGE Publishing Company

Helping educators make the greatest impact

CORWIN HAS ONE MISSION: to enhance education through intentional professional learning.

We build long-term relationships with our authors, educators, clients, and associations who partner with us to develop and continuously improve the best evidence-based practices that establish and support lifelong learning.

Solutions you want. Experts you trust. Results you need.